Cannibal
Killers

First published in 2014

A catalogue record for this book is available from the British Library

ISBN: 978-0-85733-719-1

Published by Haynes Publishing, Sparkford, Yeovil,
Somerset BA22 7JJ, UK
Tel: 01963 442030 Fax: 01963 440001
Int. tel: +44 1963 442030 Int. fax: +44 1963 440001
E-mail: sales@haynes.co.uk
Website: www.haynes.co.uk

Haynes North America Inc., 861 Lawrence Drive, Newbury Park, California 91320, USA

Images © Mirrorpix

Creative Director: Kevin Gardner
Designed for Haynes by BrainWave

Printed and bound in the US

Cannibal
Killers

From The Case Files of
 and

Claire Welch

Contents

Introduction

In April 2003, the *Mirror* revealed that human flesh might have been a regular food source for our prehistoric ancestors. The evidence was found by scientists investigating brain diseases, including BSE and its human version, variant CJD. They said it was the most likely explanation for why genes protecting against these diseases were widespread around the world. CJD was thought to be spread by proteins called prions, which assumed a dangerous new shape and damaged the brain. When rogue prions touched other prions they also changed shape, causing a chain reaction. A key aspect of prion diseases was that they could be spread by eating contaminated flesh. The consumption of beef products containing BSE prions were believed to have triggered CJD in humans.

Meanwhile, the paper also stated that Kuru, a brain disease which devastated the Fore tribe in Papua New Guinea in the first half of the 20th century, was linked with cannibalism. The research showed that mutant versions of the prion protein gene, which protects against CJD and Kuru-type diseases, appeared to have spread widely through populations as a result of natural selection. If that was the case, it suggested that in prehistoric times, cannibalism was commonplace. Professor John Collinge from University College London, who led the scientists, said: "There is extensive evidence that cannibalism is not just some rarity that happened in New Guinea."

While prehistoric ancestors practising cannibalism would be viewed as cultural rather than criminal, there are many perpetrators of this practice who have turned the act into a heinous crime. Stories like those of Stephen Griffiths, the Crossbow Cannibal who killed three sex workers in 2010, Jeffrey Dahmer, the man responsible for the deaths of 17 young men and known as the Milwaukee Cannibal, and Armin Meiwes, who advertised on the internet for a willing victim to be slaughtered and consumed in 2001, are shocking. Cannibal killers are feared the world over; their crimes whip up a media frenzy and instill fear and dread in society at large. These killers share similar traits, or have the same types of modus operandi, in which the use of knives for the maiming and mutilation of victims is commonplace.

Knives are easier to get hold of than many other types of weapons, and provide the cannibal killer with the perfect tool with which to vent extreme rage and anger at vulnerable victims, who often suffer extreme torture at the hands of the perpetrator before facing an inevitable death. Victims are often violently ripped open by their killer and many are dismembered.

Most, but not all, cannibal killers target prostitutes; the fact that these women work on the fringes of society makes them extremely vulnerable to attack. Peter Sutcliffe, the Yorkshire Ripper, mutilated and bit his victims, and it was these bite marks that led to his eventual arrest. Others prefer men, and hunt within gay communities, while there are also those that target children. Perhaps one of the worst of them all was Andrei Chikatilo, the Soviet serial killer dubbed the "Rostov Ripper", who often cannibalized his victims. Chikatilo was responsible for the deaths of at least 52 people, many of them children, who were mutilated by his teeth, knives and sticks before being strangled and battered. He had been told as a child that his older brother, who mysteriously disappeared, had been eaten by neighbours during a severe bout of famine in his home country. He eventually gave in to his own cannibalistic urges.

Cannibalism is a cultural taboo, and is committed for many reasons, including pleasure and gratification. One perpetrator who gained immense pleasure from his crimes was Albert Fish in the US. In the late 1920s he kidnapped, murdered and consumed a 10-year-old child from Manhattan. He had intended to kidnap the girl's older brother, but on his second visit to the family home chose the small child instead. Six years after his heinous crime, Fish wrote to the girl's family explaining the pleasure he had gained from consuming the child over a nine-day period. The words were read out to the child's mother, who was unable to read the chilling details for herself. The paper on which Fish wrote his confession was traced back to him, and he was executed for the crime in 1936.

In groups and tribes, cannibals have existed for thousands of years. In March 2014, the *Mirror* reported on an extreme sect living in northern India. A photographer said that people were bizarrely attracted to the group's way of life. The group, who live on the Ganges River, are known as the Aghori cannibals; they use dead bodies as beds, smear themselves with ash from cremated bodies and drink from skulls. They are feared by locals despite the fact they only eat the flesh of people who are already dead. Darragh Mason (37) spent time with the sect, which is growing in numbers, despite practising celibacy. Darragh said: "They are known to pull bodies from the Ganges and eat them. Skulls and other human bones are taken from the cremation grounds and used for ritual purposes. They believe that power comes from the dead. At one point they tried to get me to drink water from the Ganges out of a human skull but around two metres upstream they were cremating bodies so I just couldn't." The American photographer quoted above lived with the group for some time and said that more were feeling compelled to live the bizarre lifestyle. "They actively try to be thought of as the lowest in society which is why they do not dress well and their hair is often matted," he said. Despite having a terrifying reputation, the Aghori were described as "charitable" and had set up a leper colony, where they had cared for and cured 99,045 patients with full leprosy and 147,503 with partial leprosy.

In other news from March 2014, it was claimed that the oldest human footprints found outside Africa had been discovered in Norfolk; and it was thought that the first peoples in Norfolk – and the first in Britain – nearly one million years ago, could have been cannibals. The 50 footprints in question were from a man with size eight feet. Experts revealed that the prints had been made by a "Pioneer Man" (*Homo antecessor*) family foraging for food along a river estuary between 850,000 and 950,000 years ago. The extraordinary find at Happisburgh, 17 miles northeast of Norwich, was the earliest evidence of human occupation anywhere outside Africa and one of the most important archaeological discoveries ever in Britain. It shows that prehistoric ancestors first made their way to Britain 400,000 years earlier than was previously thought – when the island was still linked by land to continental Europe and the winters were far colder. The early humans may have worn clothes, built shelters and even discovered fire – again half a million years earlier than other UK finds suggest. They lived alongside hippos, mammoths, rhino and hyenas, which grazed the river valley amid dense pine forest, and used flint tools to skin and butcher bison, deer and horses for food. They supplemented their diet with shellfish, lugworms and seaweed from the tidal mudflats. But a more shocking secret of Pioneer Man's survival is that they may have eaten each other too.

Professor Chris Stringer, from the Natural History Museum in London, explained: "There is evidence of cannibalism among Pioneer Man from another 800,000-year-old site, Atapuerca in Spain. Even an eight-year-old child's remains there show butchery marks. We don't know if this was having to eat their dead fellows to survive in a crisis ... They may have done it in desperation or it may have had more sinister motives. It is known that more modern groups have eaten relatives' remains to consume their kin's knowledge and courage. More modern humans were certainly practising cannibalism. We have found evidence as recent as 14,700 years old at Cheddar Gorge in Somerset. We have human bones processed for food, tongues removed and heads specially treated. And we have found a bowl made from a human skull. It was scalped, cleaned of flesh, the eyes were cut out, then they actually trimmed it to make the bowl."

The footprint find was made by experts from the British Museum, Natural History Museum and Queen Mary University of London when, in May 2013, coastal erosion and high seas uncovered marks in packed silt on the Happisburgh foreshore. Archaeologists had been exploring the beach area for 10 years, since a man walking his dog had found an 800,000-year-old flint axe. Pioneer Man became extinct in Europe 600,000 years ago. Neanderthals appeared 200,000 years later and modern humans 40,000 years ago.

Cannibalism is still shocking the world, especially when the perpetrator devours the flesh of another human being as a result of murder, mutilation, sexual gratification and betrayal. Other cases are just as bizarre. After a raid on an eatery in Anambra, Nigeria in early 2014, police officers arrested 11 people, including the owner. The restaurant was shut down after it was found to be selling dishes made from human flesh. During the raid, police recovered at least two fresh human heads when they swooped after a tip off. The bloodied and disembodied heads were found wrapped in cellophane sheets – and police said that roasted human head was even on the menu. Two AK-47 guns, other weapons, dozens of rounds of ammunition and several mobile phones were also discovered. One local resident said: "We always saw weird people coming and going." A pastor, who was surprised to learn he had been served human flesh, complained to police. "I ate at the restaurant and the bill was very high," he told *Your Jewish News*. "The workers told me that I ate human flesh. I was shocked."

In May 1952, a storm was created by Mr W A Sibley, president of the British Vegetarian Society, when he spoke about a possible solution to the world's food shortages. He claimed that vegetarianism was a temporary solution, but that "It might fairly be argued that with the population continuing to multiply, the only ultimate solution is cannibalism. This has the virtue of tackling the problem at both ends by providing food and decreasing the population." Ten years later, a shattered human skull found in March 1962 was thought by experts to reveal cannibalism in the Thames Valley around 5,000 years ago. It was one of many finds made by a Ministry of Works team at the site of a Stone Age settlement, one and a half miles north of Staines, in what was Middlesex. Expert archaeologist Mr B Robertson-Mackay said that although the skull might have been smashed by headhunters or tomb-robbers, the most likely cause was cannibalism. It was found with another human skull and forearm among animal bones and flints in a ditch used as a food refuse dump by a settlement of farmers. They were part of a group of peoples who came over from the Continent about 3,000 BC onwards. Two ditches and a bank encircled the settlement for defence, while the entrance was via several causeways.

In November 1983 the *Mirror* commented on "the evil of video violence", arguing that sadistic and perverted films were as great a danger "to a child's mind as any infectious disease is to the body". The paper noted how children were being exposed to the "violent" videos on a daily basis and that British parents were to blame for fuelling the high street retailers' obsession with profit and greed, by purchasing them. The newspaper stated: "Adults who allow children to watch bestial sex, the dismemberment of bodies, cannibalism and torture in the privacy of the home have scaled the heights of depravity." Then in 1998, the argument concerning cannibalism reached new heights, when a TV cookery programme was blasted in May that year for showing a human placenta being eaten. Viewers complained that scenes in Channel 4's *TV Dinners*, of Hugh Fearnley-Whittingstall helping to make pâté from an afterbirth and serving it to the parents and guests was cannibalism. The Broadcasting Complaints Commission said it was unacceptable for the 8.30pm slot. Channel 4 argued that placenta was eaten in many cultures and it was not illegal in Britain, but the watchdog ruled: "The content of this programme breached a convention in a way which would have been disagreeable to many."

In 2001, Scotland Yard was considering a new animal cruelty database amid growing evidence that many killers, including cannibals, had a history of pet abuse. Experts said pet torture was a clear warning sign of a potentially violent criminal; they believed it could also be a key factor in domestic violence and child abuse. A number of murderers were known to have been vicious to animals before they turned their attentions to humans. Ian Kay, who killed a Woolworth manager in a raid – and later stabbed Yorkshire Ripper Peter Sutcliffe in Broadmoor – once fed a stray kitten to his dog. Railway rapist and multiple killer David Mulcahy bludgeoned a hedgehog to death in his school playground when he was 13. Robert Thompson, who murdered toddler James Bulger in 1993, had a long history of cruelty, and boasted that he had tied fireworks to cats' and dogs' tails. Police were urged to keep records of violence to animals that they might hear about during routine inquiries. A police source said: "Violent behaviour towards animals is often a pointer to violent behaviour towards humans. It would be relatively straightforward to compile intelligence on family pets to help to identify potentially violent individuals who do not yet have criminal convictions. One thing to watch out for would be a high turnover of pets because research shows cats or dogs in violent households often disappear, having been killed, within two years."

A survey of 57 families guilty of child neglect or abuse, conducted by child protection teams around Newcastle, found examples of animal cruelty in 88 per cent of cases. Two-thirds of the pets were attacked by bullying fathers and one-third by the abused children. In the United States, where most of the research was done, animal cruelty was a common factor amongst serial killers and spree murderers. A study in New Jersey found animal abuse in nine out of 10 households where there was violence against the children. A parent was responsible for the pet's suffering in two-thirds of cases and children in the remaining third. It was also found that 34 per cent of child victims of violence aged four to 12 had physically or sexually abused animals. Harry Fletcher, of the probation officers' union Napo, said: "There is a clear link between the torture and abuse of animals and violence against the person. It is critical that police and social services should take this link seriously and train staff. It could be the difference between life and death."

Convicted murderer and cannibal Jeffrey Dahmer was renowned for his cruelty to pets (he impaled dogs' heads on sticks) in the years leading up to his sadistic and tortuous crimes. Despite the depravity of his behaviour and his overwhelming lack of sympathy and care for victims, Dahmer was to become infamous for something else – his cult status.

In April 1994, the *Mirror* reported that: "Charles Manson, Jeffrey Dahmer, David Berkowitz ... they shocked the world with the depths of their evil, yet now the world is cashing in." The article described how public fascination with the worst murders in history had reached an all-time high, as had the temptation to make a "killing" from the men whose vicious crimes had turned them in to twisted "cult heroes". Shockingly, the market for cards, posters and songs was prolific. It seemed that nothing was taboo as long as it made money. Even the killers themselves were seizing the chance to rake in the dollars. Dahmer, the cannibal killer of Milwaukee who butchered 17 young men and ate parts of their bodies, was by the mid-1990s trying to auction off his grisly assortment of personal possessions, including the fridge where police discovered human hamburgers made from his victims. Far from being shunned, he was deluged with love letters and cash. At least £6,000 was sent to him by one woman in Chelsea, London. The paper went on to report how for £1.60 anyone in the United States could dial a dedicated telephone number and be connected to the recorded voice of John Wayne Gacy, who made his name as the biggest mass murderer on death row, where he awaited execution for his sex killings of 33 young men. Bizarrely, in between bouts of bloodletting, Gacy used to dress as Pogo the Clown to entertain neighbourhood kids in Chicago. (Gacy was a huge charity fundraiser before his capture and convictions.)

However, while he was waiting to die, Gacy's telephone message was a massive money-spinner. His paintings of clowns, created as he awaited his fate, fetched upwards of £15,000 each and were exhibited in swanky galleries from Los Angeles to Texas. Meanwhile, posters of Dahmer were snapped up by his fans, as were those of David Koresh, the cult leader who died in the infamous Waco siege in Texas. Charles Manson didn't miss out either. Axl Rose recorded a song about the man whose evil "family" massacred seven people, including the pregnant actress Sharon Tate, in 1969. Another serial killer to find himself on the end of money-making schemes was Joel Rifkin, who went on trial in Long Island in May 1994 after a three-year killing spree in which he murdered 17 prostitutes. Traffic police in the US apprehended him when he shone a torch onto his final dead victim, bound in the boot of his car. "We Love Joel" newsletters were already being circulated before the killer went on trial. Like Gacy and Dahmer, Rifkin was swamped with fan letters in his cell.

What the *Mirror* particularly objected to was the startling yardstick of America's moral decline through the "adulation of these beasts ... [in] serial killer trading cards collections ... issued with bubble gum". "Worship of these monsters", stated the paper, "appalls William Birnes, co-author of a book, *Serial Killers*." Birnes said: "Society's fascination may not create these people, but it certainly encourages them." This has been the case ever since Jack the Ripper, who despite never being named, is perhaps the most celebrated of them all: the subject of countless books, journals, articles, films, and the inspiration for many TV series and documentaries. What the fascination is that turns these killers into cult figures is the subject of much debate, but one thing is pretty clear, even into the 21st century – that the obsession with murderers, and ripper killers in particular, isn't on the wane, and cannibalism across the globe continues.

In October 2012, a story came to light about a gang of "Sweeney Todd" cannibals who murdered up to nine victims and baked some of them into pies. A court heard how police confirmed that the gang used their victims' flesh for pastries they ate themselves or sold to neighbours. Jorge Silveira (50), wife Isobel (51) and his mistress Bruna da Silva (25) lured young women to their house to work as nannies. The five-year-old daughter of one murdered woman was made to eat human flesh as part of a "purification ritual", the police claimed. Officers found the remains of Giselly da Silva (31) and Alexandra Falcao (20) buried in the garden of the trio's grisly home. The accused admitted seven further killings in Olinda, Brazil. They were said to be members of a sect that preached "purification" by reducing the world's population.

In January 2014, Ouandja Magloire, known as "Mad Dog", was identified as part of a Christian mob that dragged a man from a bus in the Central African Republic, stabbed him and used a machete to kill him. Following the incident, Magloire chopped off one of the man's legs and started chewing chunks off it before swallowing them. He said he had carried out the macabre act in revenge for the slaughter of his pregnant wife, as well as his sister-in-law and her baby in the country's capital city Bangui. The horrendous scenes were captured on video and mobile phones by eyewitnesses as others vomited in the streets. Witness Jean-Sylvestre Tchya said: "One of the individuals took hold of an arm and went and bought some bread and starting chewing on the flesh, along with his bread. The scene made many people vomit, and some cried out in horror." Another witness, Alain Gbabobou, said he watched a man wrap the head up and proclaim he would "feast on it". Magloire told the BBC he had seen his victim sitting on a minibus and decided to follow him. He ended up at the head of a 20-strong mob of youths with machetes, which had forced the bus driver to stop, then dragged the Muslim man out on the street, where he was beaten and stabbed before being set on fire.

Sectarian violence in the Central African Republic had been rife between December 2013 and January 2014. It flared up again in mid-January after the resignation of President Michel Djotodia, the first Muslim to rule the Christian majority nation. Around 1,000 lives had been lost at this point, and reports of violence echoed macabre tales linked to Jean-Bedel Bokassa, who ruled the country with an iron fist between 1966 and 1979. He was regarded by many as a brutal dictator, and was accused of eating human flesh, incorporating it in meals for visiting officials, and feeding slain opponents to animals. He died in 1996 and received a posthumous pardon in 2010.

Cannibal Killers takes a dark journey into the terrible world of these vicious serial murderers.

Somalia
(1903)

On 14th December 1903, reports which were considered well founded arrived in newspaper offices, with regard to the prevalence of cannibalism among the "Mullah's" troops. According to accounts, a native called Hugli who was executed by the group was eaten by the camp followers. The leaders then ordered the execution of some women who had taken a leading part in the orgy, and these victims too were cooked and eaten by their comrades.

The Cannibal King
(1904)

In February 1904, the *Mirror* stated: "Instances have occurred in fiction, and even in fact, of missionaries or travellers who, to save their lives, have consented to become members of a tribe of savages who would otherwise have killed them. But seldom, if ever, has a white man consented of his own free will to become not only a member, but actually the chief of a cannibal tribe."

The article continued: "Yet, in New Guinea, at the present moment, an Englishman is the 'chief of chiefs' of a ... savage tribe of Papuans and original cannibals. The man in question, the Rev. W E Bromilaw, after doing service with the Wesleyan Mission in the Fiji Islands, went out to New Guinea about 11 years ago. When he had been out six years the event occurred which led to his becoming the chief of the tribe.

"An old and distinguished chief fell ill, and the native medicine men failed to improve his condition. When at death's door – death comes rapidly in those latitudes – someone suggested the missionary. He was immediately summoned, and knowing, as all missionaries do, a good deal about medicine, he succeeded in saving the man's life. To show his intense gratitude the chief offered to make Mr Bromilaw a member of the tribe, and to admit him into a certain secret society, the membership of which carried many privileges.

"The missionary accepted the honour, and when, a short time ago, the old chief died, Mr Bromilaw was chosen to succeed him. The Rev. F W Walker, who has just come to London, after 14 years in New Guinea, knows Mr Bromilaw personally, and assured a *Daily Illustrated Mirror* representative that the 'chief' was in good health and perfectly contented with his romantic position.

"Mr Walker emphasized the fact that the society in question is social. It is in no sense religious, and any suggestion that Mr Bromilaw has accepted the beliefs of the people over whom he reigns is utterly without foundation." Whether or not Mr Bromilaw had become a cannibal was never established, but later in 1904, the shipwreck of *Aigburth* made the newspapers when seven crew members reached the coast of New Guinea in a lifeboat. The crew had been surrounded by about 60 "cannibal natives" who were "held in check with a gun" while the men retreated to another boat. They fled, leaving most of their provisions behind, and were picked up several days later. Eight other members of crew were thought to have fallen into the hands of the "natives".

"Hang King Leopold"
(1905)

In the September "Review of Reviews" in 1905, the *Mirror*'s editor, William Stead, asked: "Ought King Leopold to be hanged?" He then proposed a scheme under which the King of Belgium would be tried by the Hague Tribunal for complicity in "the Congo murders". Stead expressed his belief that the king should be executed in an interview with the Rev. John N Harris on Congo atrocities. Unfortunately for Mr Stead, the Hague Tribunal wasn't armed with the powers of an international assize court, nor was it qualified to place offenders, crowned or otherwise, in the dock. Mr Harris agreed that such a court would be "a great convenience at present". The king was accused of the torture of women in the Congo, the mutilation of children and cannibalism. The *Mirror* stated: "a whole infernal category of horrors served up with the background of cannibalism, sometimes voluntary and sometimes incredible, though it seems, enforced by the orders of the Belgian officers". Mr Stead pointed out that it was some 200 years since King Charles was beheaded, and that it was "quite time another monarch should be dismembered".

Cannibals in Serbia

(1906)

"Member of an expiring race who killed and ate his own nephew," said a headline in the *Mirror* in 1906. The newspaper wrote: "A horrible tale of cannibalism in Northern Siberia is related by the St Petersburg paper, *Nasha Shizn*. A member of the tribe of Yukagirs, an expiring people who live in the Yakutsk district, has been lodged in gaol for having killed and eaten his own nephew.

"Seven members of his family had died of starvation, and he committed the horrid deed to appease his hunger. His daughter was discovered in the very act of devouring a boiled human head."

"Cannibal People Discovered"

(1908)

In Nigeria in 1908, according to the *Mirror*, "The existence of an enormous hitherto unsuspected population of savages addicted to cannibalism has been established by the British, resident in the Bautchi Highlands district of the Nigerian Protectorate.

"In an interview with Reuter," the article continues, "Sir William Wallace, Resident-General of Northern Nigeria, stated that these people have now been made to recognize the British Administration."

Cannibal Agriculturists

(1909)

In March 1909, the *Mirror* wrote: "Naked African Savages Who Cultivate District as Lovely as Switzerland" in one of its sub-headings. It provided "a surprising account of a trip through Central Africa ... given in a report by Mr H Hesketh Bell, Governor of Uganda ... issued by the Colonial Office."

"My trip through the Bagishu country", he wrote, "filled me with amazement. We travelled for four days through enchanting scenery, and traversed a country the like of which is probably not to be seen in any other part of Africa. It is no exaggeration to state that over 80 per cent of the land is under cultivation.

"So clearly and neatly marked are the boundaries of all the plots that the countryside reminded me of the vineyards of Switzerland or of Southern France. Not only do the Bagishu eschew clothing of any sort – their district is called 'Bakedi', the Land of the Naked People – but they are addicted to cannibalism of a particularly revolting kind. They do not hunt and kill people for the sake of their flesh, but they consider that burial is a wanton waste of food."

Poetic Cannibals in Central Africa

(1912)

A missionary posted by the Plymouth Brethren to Central Africa, Daniel Crawford, returned to the UK after 23 years living amongst tribes that participated in cannibalism in Katanga country. At the YMCA in Aldersgate Street in London, he drew comparisons between life in the capital city and life in Katanga country.

"Londoners", he said, "live in a double fog – mental and atmospheric. You are, I think, becoming too materialistic; the fight for bread is getting too hard; there is no God in anything. But in Africa, they never argued about that. No cannibal for two ticks would dream of denying the existence of the Everlasting." Yet most Londoners believed that Daniel Crawford had been a prisoner of a ferocious ruler – the Emperor Mushidi – at whose capital between 10 and 20 victims were sacrificed every day to appease the blood lust of the "wicked tyrant". Slaughter went on day after day and the human skulls began "growing into hills". However, Mr Crawford continued to champion the "natives" and made many references to their "poetry of expression" and their "delightful imagery". He told the story of a young boy who learnt to read after breaking his leg: "He spends his time reading the Bible to some aged cannibals who will never be able to read themselves. The boy hates it. He yawns, and would gladly never read again; but those old cannibals make him go on, and they listen to the gospels over and over again until some phrase sticks with them and becomes part of their life."

"Englishwoman (Receives) Leg as Present"
(1912)

In November 1912, the *Mirror* covered the story of a woman who had travelled alone for over 3,000 miles in the wildest parts of the Congo. Marguerite Roby, a woman familiar with foreign travel, had just returned from the long trip, and told the *Mirror* how she had nearly died from blackwater fever and narrowly escaped death from a buffalo. When Marguerite arrived at a village close to Madiba, where there were no missionaries, she discovered that the locals had never seen a white woman before. Her appearance "caused great excitement, and eventually the chief came forward with a present" – the leg of a man who had been killed the day before. The lone traveller was horrified, and tried to make the chief understand that cannibalism was wrong and that officers would come for him. But the chief made her understand that he thought the officers would be "nice and fat". The area around Madiba was home to two tribes, the Babundas and the Bapendas, but only the latter were known to be cannibals.

In order to survive, Marguerite found her knowledge of medicine and the ability to carry out minor surgery invaluable. In Salata, these skills actually saved her life. She had just crossed a bridge when a tribe rushed at her with spears. The locals with whom she travelled called out: "Medicine Lady," and then the chief of the village came forward; he had a bad case of toothache and his face was badly swollen. "He came up to me, pointed to his face and asked: 'Could I cure his pain?'" Mrs Roby continued: "I looked into his mouth and found that he had a large abscess on the gum. Fortunately I had a small surgical knife with me, and I managed to lance the abscess very successfully. The chief was delighted and gave me several presents." On another occasion she stitched a particularly bad cut in a woman's foot and helped many tribespeople who were ill. Talking of her grave illness, Mrs Roby showed the *Mirror* an entry in her diary. It read: "July 6, 1912 – Kyembe Makula. Temp. 106.2. Think I shall peg out!"

Fritz Haarmann
(1918)

Fritz Haarmann was an unusual child, who favoured quieter activities than those of his rough and tumble peers. The Hanover-born man, however, was suspected of murdering a minimum of 27 people between 1918 and 1924. He was found to have committed at least 24 murders and was described as a man "who picked his victims from male prostitutes, runaways and even young male commuters". He lured his victims to his apartment for sex before biting through their throats in order to kill them. Dubbed the Vampire of Hanover, he was known to have dismembered the men and teenagers he killed before partially eating them. Body parts that were discarded were found in the Leine River, but the "meat" of several victims was sold on the black market as "canned pork", a trade in which he had been participating before he murdered his victims. Haarmann was finally placed under police surveillance in 1924. When officers found him trying to lure a young boy, they arrested him. Once in police custody he claimed he had killed somewhere between 50 and 70 young men, whom he had cannibalized.

Haarmann was referred to in court as a "werewolf" and a "vampire", and the details of his crimes included rape and mutilation. The case caused a sensation in Germany, and the country waited for the trial's outcome with bated breath. He was sentenced to death and died by guillotine in April 1925. Although the term "serial killer" had not yet been coined, Haarmann was surely one of the most notorious in Germany.

Cannibal Murder
(1930)

The *Mirror* reported on 3rd June 1930 that the murder of a father and son included the suggestion that the younger victim was "eaten by natives in the New Hebrides" (which is now part of Vanuatu). The Probate Court, presided over by Mr Justice Hill, was asked to make a grant in the estate valued at £2,500 of John Lautour, who had emigrated to the South Pacific. In 1874 the man's son was born, but the pair were murdered on 8th September 1890 in the village in which they lived. The reason the case came to court was because it was impossible to establish whether or not the testator predeceased his son, whom he had made his heir. As a result, it was "submitted that the property disposed of by his will of 1891 devolved in an intestacy upon the testator's father, William Francis Joseph Young, as next of kin". The judge granted the application.

Leonarda Cianciulli
(1939)

Leonarda Cianciulli, from Montella, Italy, was a disturbed child who twice attempted suicide. Of her numerous pregnancies once she was married, 10 of her children died. When she heard that her oldest surviving son, Giuseppe, was to join the Italian Army and fight in the Second World War, she was convinced that the only thing that would keep him safe was human sacrifice. She planned the murder of three women whom she invited to her home, then murdered them with an axe before cutting their bodies into pieces. Cianciulli threw these pieces in a pot, dissolved them in caustic soda and poured the thick liquid into a septic tank. She retained the blood and once it had coagulated she dried it, before grinding it and mixing it with everyday foods – including teacakes which she served to other women who came to visit. During her confession she admitted that she and her son had also eaten these cakes. The third victim, described by the murderer as "fat and white", had her body parts boiled and mixed with cologne to make a soap, which Cianciulli then gave to neighbours and acquaintances.

A neighbour who was suspicious of Cianciulli alerted the police, and the disturbed mother admitted her crimes immediately. She was found guilty and sentenced to 30 years in prison. Her final three years were spent in a criminal asylum, where she died in 1970. The pot in which the victims' body parts were boiled is now housed in the Criminological Museum, Rome.

"Cannibalism" in Hong Kong
(1945)

A Royal Artilleryman, Warrant-Officer Tollison, gave an interview in Vancouver in October 1945, in which he said that small children wandering around Hong Kong's streets were in danger of being captured and eaten. The officer, one of 600 British prisoners "on the way home", said: "Officials warned the people to keep their children off the streets because of wild dogs, but it wasn't wild dogs, it was cannibalism."

Takehiko Tazaki

(1945)

Lieutenant Takehiko Tazaki confessed to eating parts of a dead Australian soldier in December 1945. He was sentenced to death by hanging by a court martial in Wewak, New Guinea. Tazaki had pleaded that he was very hungry and wanted to restore his strength. Declaring that cannibalism was not a crime, Mr F M Forde, the Australian Army Minister, announced after sentencing that the death penalty passed on the starving Japanese soldier had been commuted to five years' imprisonment.

In August 1992, it was revealed in the *Mirror* that Japanese soldiers regularly ate Prisoners of War in the jungle during the Second World War. More than 100 Australians and Indians – some of whom were still alive at the time – were victims of cannibalism in New Guinea. A Tokyo professor who studied secret papers claimed the horror was "hushed up" after the war.

Joachim Kroll

(1955)

A German, Joachim Kroll, began his killing spree in 1955. He left the police in no doubt that they were looking for a cannibal – all his victims were skinned. Kroll's modus operandi was to surprise his victims before strangling them and performing sexual acts upon the bodies. He would then mutilate his victims, cutting off pieces to consume. In early July 1976 he was arrested for the death of a four-year-old child, Marion Kettner, when police found the girl's dismembered body at the killer's home. A neighbour who was constantly plagued by Kroll's blocked plumbing system had become suspicious. Marion had suffered a horrendous ordeal, and when police arrived they found one of her tiny hands cooking on a small stove. Some of her body parts were discovered in the fridge, while her entrails were stuck in the waste-disposal pipe.

On his arrest, Kroll confessed to 13 further murders. The German media dubbed him the "Ruhr Cannibal", while the public heard how he had often eaten human flesh to save money on his shopping. He was convicted and sentenced to life imprisonment. He died in 1991, while still incarcerated.

Ed Gein
(1957)

"A dramatic question was put to farmer Edward Gein today," wrote the *Mirror* on 19th November 1957. "Did you eat five women?" Hollow-eyed, round-shouldered Gin (51), a bachelor, found himself opposite District Attorney Earl Kileen. Police had called at Gein's lonely farm in Wisconsin in their search for Mrs Bernice Worden (58), who had been missing from her hardware store in Plainfield for a few days. They found her – headless, and hanging by the heels from the farm's kitchen ceiling. Gein was said to have told police: "I've been killing for seven years." Then, according to Mr Kileen, he opened a box and produced five women's skulls.

Mr Kileen asked him: "Did you intend to eat Mrs Worden?" Gein was alleged to have replied: "I can't remember." According to American publication *BUP*, the skulls and bones of five more people were found in the "house of horror". "It looks like cannibalism," said the District Attorney. In three hours of questioning, Gein told the police that he robbed graves to get the skulls and bones. Under heavy guard, he was taken to the county jail for further questioning. Wearing faded green trousers, a cap and a jacket, he plodded through heavy snow to a police car. Police said he was going to take them to the place where he claimed he had dug up the skulls. Lamps and chairs were taken from the farm for testing – to see if their coverings consisted of human skin.

Police had first gone to see Gein because he had been heard to say that he intended buying antifreeze mixture at Mrs Worden's shop, and the receipt for the item was the last one found on the counter; the last item she had sold before closing the shop that day. The cash register was missing, and it was said to have been found in the farmer's bedroom; he was duly charged with theft. Meanwhile, the search of his nine-roomed house continued. In addition, all cold cases in the Wisconsin area were re-examined.

The following day, after questioning by the District Attorney, Gein was ordered to undergo lie detector tests. Police hoped that these would solve the question of whether Gein was a cannibal or not. By this time, he was alleged to have confessed to killing Mrs Worden while "in a daze". Mr Kileen said: "Gein declares that he didn't eat Mrs Worden. We must have a lie detector test on that." He said that Gein had claimed that he had dug the skulls from a cemetery for a thrill. But police doubted the story, especially when they identified one of the skulls as that of Mrs Mary Hogan, who had gone missing in 1954. Mr Kileen said that her body had never been found, "so she couldn't have been buried in a cemetery. It is more likely that she met her death by violence." Detectives also claimed that at least one chair at Gein's "sagging farmhouse" had been upholstered with human skin.

New "horrors" were discovered on 21st November 1957 in what was dubbed the "House of Skulls". Police escorted the farmer's newly appointed defence lawyer, William Beiter, to the ramshackle farm, just six miles from Plainfield. While there, the police told him that they had found portions of 15 bodies. They showed Mr Beiter the death masks and four chairs covered with human skin. According to police reports, the "death masks" were mounted on wooden bases, like hunting trophies, and hung on stairways and walls. In addition, they showed the lawyer a drum made from human skin.

That same day, Gein was charged with the first-degree murder of Mrs Bernice Worden. The farmer pleaded "insanity". Judge Boyd Clark ruled he should be held for trial, and the prosecution, according to Reuter, did not oppose a move to have Gein mentally examined. The defendant was also alleged to have admitted to killing tavern owner Mary Hogan, but appeared in court for just five minutes. Conviction for first-degree murder charges carried a life sentence in Wisconsin.

On 22nd November 1957, Edward Gein was sent to a criminal asylum "for observation". He was convicted in 1968 of the murder of Bernice Worden – she had been shot and trussed up like a wild deer – and sentenced to life imprisonment, which he served in a secure hospital.

It transpired after his incarceration that Gein had been devoted to his mother, Augusta, who had bought the farm as a means of protecting her two sons from influences outside the home. Gein's father died in 1940 from alcoholism, and his mother spent hours and hours telling her sons about the immorality of life. There was some suggestion that Gein killed his older brother for moaning about their mother's incessant need to "preach" to them, and her reading of graphic verses from the Old Testament. Gein was distraught when his mother died in 1945, and lived as a recluse until he was sentenced to life imprisonment. He died in 1984 aged 78, and is buried next to his only friend, his mother.

"Cannibals Eat Village Policeman"
(1959)

On 19th May 1959, a group of "cannibal tribesmen" raided Matuari Village, in a primitive district of New Guinea, and killed and ate the policeman, it was claimed. Brigadier D M Cleland, Administrator of New Guinea, said it was the first reported case of cannibalism in the district for almost three years. The brigadier added that after eating the policeman, the cannibals chased the remaining villagers to a petroleum company's camp at nearby Bwata. The tribesmen then retreated to the hills. Mr W Dishon, Senior Officer for "Native Affairs", said the policeman's job was to report to the administration signs of any trouble in the area.

"Wanted in a Cooking Pot"
(1959)

"Tell me," said the Queen Mother on a trip to Kenya in 1959, "what became of the cannibals?" Ewart Grogan replied: "Ma'am, we don't have cannibals now. We have bank managers." The Queen Mother was meeting the world's top "expert" on cannibals, who himself had only just managed to escape from the cooking pot. Grogan had been the first white man to make the overland trek from the Cape to Cairo at the turn of the 20th century. It was a time when Africa was being "opened up", according to the *Mirror* – when people had told Grogan to be careful of cannibal tribes. Believing he had nothing to fear while travelling through the continent, he stumbled on a "cannibal feast", finding the leftovers of a meal beside a cooking pot. He was sickened by the "dreadful" sight, and the vultures circling overhead. The paper stated: "Even his native bearers were put off their own food for days." Grogan and his small party were attacked by the cannibal tribesmen, but he scattered them with volleys from his double-barrelled rifle. He then fled for his life. Grogan later discovered that for mile upon mile the rivers ran with blood and corpses floated close to the banks. Grogan wrote a book about his experiences in Africa, *The Man From The Cape*, telling how, as a young man, he made his cross-continent trek to win a wife.

North Katanga, Congo
(1960)

"United Nations troops, menaced by growing bands of savage tribesmen, began pulling out of trouble spots in North Katanga, Congo, yesterday," wrote the *Mirror* on 16th November 1960. Patrols of Irish and Ethiopian troops, who were stationed in UN-controlled areas for several weeks, had arrived back at their headquarters in Albertville. A UN spokesman declined to give an official reason for the mass withdrawal, but he admitted that the UN had to revise its methods of operation against the tribesmen.

He said that Irish troops had been withdrawn completely from the Niemba area, which just the week before had been the scene of an ambush of 11 Irish soldiers. Nine men had been killed and two were wounded. Eight bodies were recovered, but they eventually called off the search for the ninth. Officials believed the victim had been cannibalized. It is thought that the Irish soldier showed so much courage on the battlefield that the tribesmen ate him in order to gain the same courage that he displayed. "He was a brave man. His flesh will give our brothers great power," one tribesman was quoted as saying.

Stone Age Territory
(1962)

Writing in the *Mirror* from New Guinea in July 1962, a journalist stated: "Naked, with bird-of-paradise feathers stuck in his hairnet, he felt me all over, grunted quickly three times and smiled." He continued: "I was with the Dani tribe, some of 400,000 (out of 700,000) Papuans in this Dutch colony. They live in valleys along the central mountain backbone. Under tall sighing trees I sat in a hut, blinded by the smoke of an open fire on which roasted a heap of sweet potatoes.

"Opposite, a man with no face gibbered at me. When young he had raped and, as punishment, been held face down in a fire. I WAS BACK IN THE STONE AGE. TIME HAD STOOD STILL FOR THE DANI. They still use stone axes. They saw their first non-Dani less than four years ago when the Dutch came."

Up to this point, the tribe had never seen a wheel and had not used anything except a pointed stick to paddle their rafts and till their land. A good, hard-working woman was rated as worth one pig. The Dani had retained their customs for centuries. Chased out of their East Indies islands when 95 million Indonesians became independent in 1949, the Dutch "stuck fast" to neglected New Guinea as a last "toehold". With the Indonesian president, Sukarno, they agreed to discuss the future of the territory the following year, but negotiations stalled.

Mr Kendau Gebze, a member of the Papuan parliament, said: "If the Indonesians come we will eat them as we ate the Japs in World War II." Since mid-January 1962, around 1,000 West Indonesians had landed in West Irian, which Sukarno called New Guinea. Half were known to have been captured by the Dutch, killed or cannibalized by the islanders. Bitter prisoners told how they were convinced they would be welcomed, and they had been, but as "extra portions" rather than as a people that could live side by side with tribespeople. Sukarno was described as a virtual dictator and there were at least four attempts on his life. Despite the fact that the Dutch had spent £10 million on the area each year, most of the officials had left. The fate of the Dani was left undecided.

Tribesmen in the Congo Shock the West

(1967)

A report that Westerners were being eaten by tribesmen in the Congo shocked the West on 12th July 1967. The report came from the American news agency Associated Press, which said that cannibalism had broken out in Lubumbashi in the strife-torn Katanga province. Congo Interior Minister Etienne Tshishekedi was quoted as saying: "The life of white settlers in Lubumbashi is in danger. Several of them have been eaten by Congolese. I ordered the local population to stop such barbarism and reprisals. I am going to Bukavu, where similar acts could take place – all the more since the local population is still furious against the mercenaries who mutinied there."

Four hours later, this report was denied by the Congolese Embassy in Paris. Officials admitted in a statement that "some malicious acts" had been committed by some Congolese on foreigners, but added: "The Minister never mentioned any acts of cannibalism at Lubumbashi in his declaration." One thing that was clear as Western embassies investigated the report was that cannibalism was still practised in the Congo. The *Mirror* wrote: "This may seem too incredible to believe to western nations where a cannibal is just half-remembered fiction out of Robinson Crusoe, or the creation of a cartoonist's pen. But there are, in fact, many more victims of cannibalism than the cartoonist's missionary trussed up in a bubbling pot. In the vast and primitive Congo, where civilized believers are less than paper tissue thin, two British volunteers of the Katanga Army were slaughtered and eaten after an attack by tribesmen."

There were also repeated reports from the area about an armed band of "Leopard Men" who ate the hearts of their victims, while in Nigeria, one of Africa's then most progressive nations, there was an outbreak of cannibalism in 1960. Some 27 men, including a priest, were accused of eating two victims. Meanwhile in New Guinea, 16 tribesmen stood trial accused of eating their enemies. The *Mirror* wrote: "Cannibalism has not always been treated mainly as a joke in the West. The word itself comes from the Spanish 'Canibales' – a 17th-century version of the name given to the notorious man-eating Carib Indians, discovered by the Spaniards in the New World.

"The Victorian era empire-building of many nations came across cannibalism from the Eskimo regions of the Far North to the natives of New Zealand. They fought it with the Bible ... and bullets." The newspaper continues: "Unfortunately, as we can see, they failed to stamp it out completely. In fact in New Zealand there was cannibalism as recently as 1883. A man was tried and hanged for this ultimate crime. And in the Pacific Island of Fiji, where most ferocious cannibals once lived, the children still sing a rhyme about a British missionary killed and eaten in 1867." It ran: "Oh, dead is Mr Baker. They killed him on the road, And they ate him, boots and all."

At the time, there were two main theories why people became cannibals. One was that many tribes believed that once they had eaten their victim, they would assume his best qualities, while the other held by some scientists was that people turned cannibal because they lacked the protein normally gained from other meat in their diets. The *Mirror* continued: "Cannibalism, of course, revolts most people, but according to one white woman who accidentally sampled human flesh in 1964, it tasted quite good." However, the newspaper said: "A sour thought really in a civilized world which prefers its cannibals in cartoons, not in the news columns."

Man Eats Wife and Children

(1967)

Mahola Petikite (55) killed his wife, his three children and his father by witchcraft and then ate them, a court was told in 1967. The court in Dar-es-Salaam, Tanzania, listened in horror to Petikite's confession and explanation, in which he said he did not know he had committed a crime. His urge for human flesh came after he took "native medicine", but with no family left he felt his health had failed, and he visited a witch doctor who immediately called in the police. Petikite pleaded guilty to possessing witchcraft instruments, and was remanded in custody to await a decision on whether he should face trial for mass murder or practising witchcraft.

"Death-case Man says: 'I am a Cannibal'"

(1970)

In July 1970 a young man was charged with murder after he told a policeman: "I have a problem. I am a cannibal." Police arrested him and another man in Salinas, California, after they found human finger bones in their pockets. The charges followed the discovery of a headless and heartless body of a camper in the Yellowstone National Park in Montana. Police said that one of the men, believed to be a member of a satanic cult, told them he had eaten the flesh from the fingers and cut the victim's heart out and eaten it.

Stanley Baker (22) and Harry Stoup (29), both from Wyoming, were questioned by a highway patrol officer when they were arrested after a traffic accident near Salinas. The camper was identified as James Schlosser, a Montana social worker, and the car, driven by Baker and Stoup, was registered in his name. Police said that Baker, who admitted he was "a cannibal", told them he had shot Schlosser and then cut the body into pieces with a knife.

Robert Maudsley

(1974)

Robert Maudsley was first convicted for his crimes in 1974, but the Broadmoor patient – who killed another inmate – warned a judge in October 1977: "I'll do it again if you send me back." David Cheeseman (32) and Maudsley (24) admitted at Reading Crown Court to garroting 26-year-old David Francis with a length of flex. Both were jailed for life, but on 16th March 1979, four-time killer Maudsley went back to prison for the rest of his life.

There was a life "stretching before him like a caged animal for perhaps another 50 years," said his counsel. But the judge at Leeds Crown Court was unmoved. "At present I see no reason why you should ever be released," he told Maudsley, who admitted murdering two fellow prisoners at Wakefield top security prison. Earlier the court heard that Maudsley, described as homosexual, was sent to Broadmoor in 1974 after killing a lover. In 1977 he strangled another patient and was sent to Wakefield. In July 1978 he stabbed and garroted a prisoner in his cell, then calmly went for lunch. On his way back to his cell he fatally stabbed another prisoner. Defence counsel Edward Lyons, QC, said that when Maudsley was a boy, his father locked him up for six months and beat him twice a day. "When he's killing, he's thinking of his father," said Mr Lyons.

An article in the *Mirror* in November 1981 said: "Cages are being used in jails to keep Britain's most dangerous killers away from other prisoners." The Home Office revealed that the cages had been built about three years earlier, and were being used at several prisons for solitary confinement. Multiple killer Maudsley was caged at Wakefield for more than three years. In October 1996, the press reported that a barber was called into jail to cut Maudsley's waist-length hair, after 12 years' growth. Warders were too terrified to go near the killer with scissors, it was claimed. Dubbed "Hannibal the Cannibal", Maudsley was known, by this time, to have eaten the brains of one of his victims. He agreed to let the barber cut his hair to shoulder length.

In June 2004, the *Mirror* reported that after 26 years in solitary confinement Maudsley, one of Britain's most notorious serial killers, was close to death. The cannibal was said to have suffered dramatic weight loss, because drugs given to control his violent mood swings dulled his appetite to such an extent that he could barely eat. The killer's skin was said to be peeling in an allergic reaction to chemicals that were being pumped into his skeletal body. A doctor was visiting him twice a day at his two-room glass cage. Insiders at Wakefield jail claimed that Maudsley had lost the will to live because of a punishing regime of almost total isolation. One said: "He is a shocking weight. Concerns are growing for his health. He is skin and bone." The source continued: "He hardly ever gets out to exercise so his skin is a deathly white, like tissue paper. He refused to have his hair cut and he can't even be bothered to put his false teeth in. He was a dangerous killer but I doubt he is a threat to anyone now. It is hard to feel sorry for such a man. But it's still shocking to see him like that. He appears to have been beaten by his regime. It's as if he knows he is going to meet his maker."

When Maudsley killed a paedophile in Broadmoor, according to a guard at the secure hospital, he cracked the man's skull open "like a boiled egg" and ate part of the victim's brain with a spoon.

Maudsley, who loved classical music, poetry and art, was known to have a genius-level IQ, although no one could ever explain his murderous rages. He once described solitary confinement in his 10-foot square cell as "like being buried alive in a concrete coffin". In July 2006, Maudsley set a new UK record of 28 years for the longest time spent in solitary confinement. The then 53-year-old was locked in his confined cell for up to 23 hours a day after the death of fellow inmate William Roberts. He was only allowed to exercise for an hour a day, accompanied by six prison guards. One insider said: "He has learned to get on with it. He'll never see life outside the four walls of his cell." Later that year, Maudsley spent his 29th Christmas alone in jail. A Prison Service source reiterated: "Nearly 29 consecutive years would be unbearable for most people, but somehow he has learned to get on with it. It is a record which is likely to stand for a very long time."

In 2010, Maudsley was said to have asked if he could play board games with prison staff – because he was so bored. A report described him as willing to engage with staff after years of sullen resentment, but it added: "He has hostile thoughts ... and urges to kill or harm others." One officer said: "There isn't exactly a long queue for that first game of Scrabble."

Ottis Toole
(1976 onwards)

Working alongside serial killer Henry Lee Lucas, Ottis Toole would eventually admit to hundreds of unsolved murders over several decades, involving murder, arson and cannibalism. Toole started his criminal activities with arson and later confessed he was sexually aroused by the act. When he met Lucas at a soup kitchen in 1976 he was already a prolific criminal. The two men developed a sexual relationship which would lead to serial killings, and while Toole would later give graphic accounts of cannibalism, Lucas never did. Toole claimed that the pair committed more than 100 murders, but went on to help police recover the bodies of over 245 missing people. By the time the police finished investigating the crimes of the two men, the victim count was nearer to 500.

Toole gave an interview on cannibalism to an American tabloid and went into quite a lot of detail about cooking and eating human flesh, which he enjoyed with his homemade barbecue sauce.

President Amin
(1977)

On 27th April 1977 President Amin was accused of cannibalism. Amin's former personal doctor said the Ugandan dictator ate part of the liver from one of his dead ministers, in the belief that this would ward off evil spirits. The accusation was made at a House of Commons meeting by Dr John Kibukamusoke, who fled from Uganda in 1973. He said the horrifying act was uncovered when fishermen found the body of Foreign Minister Michael Ondaga floating in the Nile after he disappeared. They saw that his liver was missing, and the doctor said it was later learned that the minister's liver had been taken to Amin's command post, where he ate part of it. The doctor explained that Amin was very superstitious – and the Kakwa tribe to which he belonged believed strongly in revenge after death. He said: "They also believe that if you eat a piece of your victim's liver, his evil spirits will not haunt you." The doctor, who was the dictator's personal physician for three years, listed a series of murders of prominent Ugandans blamed on Amin. They were mainly people that Amin imagined were opposed to him.

The doctor said that Amin suffered from hypermania – streams of ideas which come one after the other and lead to confusion. Amin, the doctor claimed, also suffered from an inferiority complex and paranoia, which made him turn violently against people around him. He urged MPs to wage a trade boycott, and called for Amin to be banned from the Commonwealth conference to be held in London in June 1977. The only way to remove Amin from power was to isolate him from the rest of the world, said the doctor, who was by now Professor of Medicine at Zambia University.

Nikolai Dzhumagaliev
(1979)

There were no outward signs that Russian-born Nikolai Dzhumagaliev was a serial killer and cannibal, but in 1979, he began "ridding" the world of "undesirable" sex workers. Seven women are known to have been killed by Dzhumagaliev, but estimates put victim numbers at closer to 100. Dubbed "Metal Fang" by the press for his white metal teeth, the killer lured unsuspecting victims into parks before raping them and killing them with an axe. He then cooked some body parts of his victims and ate them. He served human flesh to his friends at dinner parties, and was viewed by his associates as a quiet, softly spoken gentleman. He was eventually caught when two guests invited for dinner discovered a woman's head and other body parts in his fridge. Dzhumagaliev was convicted for his crimes and found to be insane. He spent time in a secure psychiatric hospital, but escaped from custody for two years between 1989 and 1991. After recapture he served another 10 years. Eventually he was released into the care of his family in Eastern Europe, but he was free to travel the world ...

Bokassa – A Ruler's Shame

(1979)

Emperor Bokassa was present at the massacre of a hundred children in the Central African Empire, a leading French newspaper claimed on 21st May 1979. The paper, *Le Monde*, quoted a woman who said she had spoken to survivors. She said: "According to all the accounts, Emperor Bokassa was at the massacre." Amnesty International claimed the children were beaten, stabbed and stoned to death for demonstrating against a new rule that they should wear school uniforms.

In July 1979, the *Mirror* reported that the "savage tyrant" had been overthrown. Bokassa, whose name means butcher's boy, was toppled from power after 13 terror-filled years as head of the Central African Empire. During his bloody rule, he had the bodies of tortured rivals thrown to crocodiles. The coup on 21st July was a bloodless one, however. Bokassa was overthrown by his nephew David Dacko while on a money-scrounging visit to Libya. Bokassa later left Tripoli and flew to Paris, but after being refused permission to land at Orly, his plane finally touched down in Normandy. No one on board was allowed to leave the aircraft.

Earlier that day, the revolt had brought people dancing into the streets. But the French Government was soon forced to rush in troops from nearby Gabon as the celebrations turned into widespread looting.

Bokassa, a former French Army captain, had ruled with hate from the day he snatched power in 1966. His first task was to smash the spine of the army chief who led his takeover assault, in case he became a threat. During the years that followed most Western powers were well aware that Bokassa was a mass-murderer, but nobody raised a finger to stop him. The French, who still controlled the country's economy, even "helped" when he crowned himself "emperor" in a scandalous £20 million ceremony in 1977, but Bokassa, who liked to call himself the "Black Napoleon", overstepped the mark with the massacre of 100 children. He was accused of cannibalism by the new rulers of his former country, who claimed they had found human bodies in a freezer at his palace. An official of the new government said the bodies had been cut up for human consumption. Meanwhile, the Black Napoleon found refuge on the Ivory Coast.

In November 1979, the *Mirror*'s Peter Stephens wrote: "Dining with big-shots in exotic African places to the distant thud of tom toms can lead to severe delayed indigestion. My tummy felt distinctly queasy after newly installed President David Dacko made a dramatic radio announcement in the Central African Republic. He claimed that his predecessor, the sinister Emperor Bokassa, was a cannibal as well as being a torturer and murderer. And that the sinister little man had shared his ghastly 'delicacies' with unsuspecting guests. Now where does that leave me I wonder? For I was twice a guest at Bokassa's palace in the capital of Bangui. The food seemed normal enough. The meat was perhaps a bit rare for my taste. But I'm pretty sure I was served lamb chops on both occasions and you can't mistake that for something else. Or can you? I'm not taking any more chances. Next time I'm in that part of the world I shall go vegetarian."

On 19th December 1986, former Emperor Bokassa went on trial in his absence in Bangui, accused of cannibalism and the massacre of 100 children. The string of crimes with which he was charged could ultimately lead him to the gallows. Jean-Bedel Bokassa had made his way voluntarily back to the shabby capital of Bangui, where he once sat on a golden throne. The fallen ruler, in contrast, sat in a sweltering courtroom accused of torture, murder and cannibalism. The 65-year-old had already been convicted and sentenced to death in his absence for crimes during his 13-year reign, but the power-mad tyrant who hero-worshipped Napoleon returned from exile to answer his accusers.

Stephens wrote: "I last saw Bokassa over dinner at his fabulous castle in Bangui. The Emperor wore a dress uniform with rows of medals hanging down almost to his knees, and diamond-studded black suede shoes. He carried a diamond-studded key." He had succumbed to power mania, and his excesses began following the bizarre ceremony in 1977. He was also a very cruel man. He once ordered thieves and robbers to be dragged out of the local jail and into the town square, then led a vicious attack on the helpless victims, leaving three dead and 46 badly injured. As he grew more pompous, Bokassa issued court edicts. Stephens continued: "Everyone who approached the august presence had to halt six yards away and bow. His beautiful wife Catherine had to be given the same regal treatment. He called the aloof General de Gaulle 'Papa' and was on friendly terms with Giscard d'Estaing, the French President – a relationship both were bitterly to regret.

"Bokassa gave Giscard presents of diamonds from the rich mines in his country. It caused a scandal which helped unseat Giscard in the 1981 election. By then, Giscard had sent paratroopers to overthrow him. Bokassa helped himself to diamonds from his mines and kept a huge glass jar of them on his desk. Any visitor who pleased or impressed him often found a fistful of diamonds suddenly thrust at him. He took personal charge of everything. Plumbers, carpenters and electricians would get phone calls to come and fix something in his castle. Once he phoned a Paris shop from Bangui and asked them to send someone – at his expense – to show him how to work a £500 video recorder he had bought. They did, and the man found that Bokassa had forgotten to plug it in.

"He was thrilled with any decoration. In 1970, he was delighted when he was decorated as 'a Knight of the Brotherhood of Stamp Collectors' in Paris. But his ugly nature was never far below the surface. He drank. His favourite tipple was Beaujolais, and he started on it at 10.30 every morning. A servant would appear in his office bearing a silver tray in his white-gloved hands with a bottle of wine – and drink a glass first to make sure it was not poisoned."

It was Bokassa's drunkenness that led him to vicious attacks, usually on innocent people. There was wholesale torture, and he raided the country's coffers to buy three castles in France and properties in other countries. His former chef claimed in March 1987 that the former emperor ate human flesh washed down with Beaujolais. The chef said that the meat had to be "flamed with gin" before being served to him.

Dennis Nilsen
(1983)

In February 1983 it was reported that 17 people were believed to have been butchered by a mass murderer. All the victims were thought to be young male "down and outs". They had been strangled. A grisly search for the remains of the victims was underway on 10th February 1983 after two heads and a hand were discovered at 23 Cranley Gardens, Muswell Hill, North London. A further 14 victims were believed to have been murdered three miles away at 195 Melrose

Avenue, Willesden Green. A man was being questioned by police.

The first victim was thought to have been murdered five years previously, while the last victim was thought to have died no more than three weeks before the police find. Police had first been alerted a few days earlier, when a plumber found the rotting remains of three adults blocking a drain at the house in Cranley Gardens. More remains were found on 10th February as detectives dug up the garden, stripped woodwork and tore up floorboards. A full-scale search of the house and garden at Melrose Avenue was due to begin in earnest. A workman loading scaffolding said: "Police said they're prepared to take the whole building apart if need be." Detectives believed the victims, mostly tramps and down and outs, met their killer in local pubs. He then offered them a bed for the night before strangling them. The bodies were then cut up and boiled. Some parts were flushed down the toilet and others buried in the garden or hidden in the house. One of the dead was identified as Stephen Neil Sinclair (20), of no fixed address. Police believed the killings could have been carried out by a homosexual, or somebody with a grudge against them. The man helping with inquiries was named as former policeman Dennis Nilsen.

On 11th February 1983, Dennis Andrew Nilsen (37) was charged with murdering Stephen Sinclair. The ex-army cook was charged at Hornsey police station, where he had been taken for questioning soon after the first body parts had been discovered. Nilsen, a £7,000-a-year executive officer at a job centre in Kentish Town, was due to appear before Highgate magistrates.

Crowds gathered as the diggers moved in. Seven policemen, looking uncomfortable in bright green boiler suits and wellingtons, carried spades, sieves, rakes and a wad of black plastic bags. This said it all: it was simple equipment, but all that was necessary to unearth the 14 bodies that were believed to be buried in the unkempt back garden in Melrose Avenue. Nobody spoke as the police marched briskly down the side of the Victorian semi. A crowd of more than 60 people began to disperse as the officers arrived, and as scaffolding and blue plastic covers shielded the scene from the public. One witness told a journalist that a man living at the property used to have bonfires at all hours until the council put a stop to them. After four hours of digging the police left, apparently having found nothing. Journalists from across the globe began to descend on the street, and TV crews from France, Australia and the US aimed their cameras at what became dubbed the "House of Horrors".

Meanwhile the press interviewed Nilsen's elderly mother, who held her head in her hands as she talked about her son. She hadn't seen him for 10 years, after he returned from service abroad with the army. He had spent a year with the Metropolitan Police before becoming a civil servant. Betty Scott, who remarried after divorcing Nilsen's father, still lived in Aberdeenshire where her son had been born. Mrs Scott had brought up her three children without the help of her Norwegian husband, who she claimed was rarely there. Nilsen had done well at art, and everyone assumed he was destined for a career in that subject, until he came home from school and announced he wanted to join the army. He became a boy soldier. His brother, Olav, said that the family hadn't seen Nilsen for about nine years, following a "silly family row". Before leaving the army, Nilsen served briefly in the Catering Corps attached to the Queen's Guards at Ballater, near Balmoral. Nilsen was said to have left the police as a cadet because he was unhappy with the pay.

Nilsen's pet dog Bleep was meanwhile sent to Battersea Dogs' Home in South London. Officials at the home said the border collie cross was about eight years old and blind in one eye. She appeared to be pining for her master, but was moved to the home's country kennels at Windsor, where she would stay until her long-term future was decided.

The newspapers soon announced that human remains had been found in plastic bags only a few hundred yards from the house in Melrose Avenue 18 months earlier. Medical graduate Robert Wilson (26) was walking his dog along Dollis Hill Lane in August 1981 when he found a bag lying on the pavement near a lamp-post rubbish bin. Parts of what appeared to be human remains were spilling out, and Mr Wilson called Kilburn police, who took away a number of bags found in the area. The victim was never identified.

Stephen Sinclair was described as a "wanderer", who had left his home in Scotland several years before. After he left the village of St Martin's near Perth, he never contacted his adoptive family again.

Following Nilsen's one-minute hearing at Highgate court, where he was remanded, police cadets found fragments of smashed skulls in a "gruesome" burial patch at the house in Melrose Avenue, on the second day that they had made a fingertip search of the waste ground behind the house. Police said it was the most "significant" find yet. Soon other pieces of bone and a dental plate were dug up.

By this time, police had a list of possible victims dating back five years. One was thought to be a 26-year-old Canadian student, Ken Ockenden, who had vanished from a London hotel in 1979, but Detective Chief Superintendent Geoffrey Chambers said: "It is doubtful if we will ever be able to identify all the dead."

The month after Nilsen's arrest, Bleep pined to death for him. Two months later, in May 1983, Nilsen faced four new murder charges. The victims were said to have been young men. He was also accused of two attempted murders, and was read all the charges in a cell at Highgate court shortly before his 16th weekly appearance there. The four new charges all related to alleged killings at Melrose Avenue, including Kenneth James Ockenden in 1979, unemployed teenager Martyn Brandon Duffey, from Cheshire, in 1980, Scotsman William David Sutherland, from Edinburgh, in 1980 and Malcolm Barlow, from Rotherham, Yorkshire, in 1981. The murder attempts were said to have been committed against unemployed barman Douglas Stewart from Wick at Melrose Avenue in November 1980 and student Paul Nobbs of Bushey, Hertfordshire, at Cranley Gardens in November 1981. Nilsen was remanded in custody for another week, and there was no application for bail.

Nilsen was committed for trial at the Old Bailey on 26th May 1983. He was granted an extension of legal aid so that counsel could work on the case. By October, Nilsen had confessed to the slaughter of 16 men. By day, Nilsen was a respected civil servant and union official, but by night, it was alleged, he was a frenzied killer of the unsuspecting young drifters he picked up in pubs. He was alleged to have told police that he felt like a "quasi-god", who lured his victims with offers of food and drink. They were then strangled with his neckties and their bodies were butchered, boiled or burned. Prosecutor Allan Green told the Old Bailey that the gruesome killings at two North London addresses were spread over four years. Some of the victims were homosexual; some were male prostitutes. Nilsen told the police that he was "emotionally homosexual" himself, but he denied any sexual motive for the bloodshed. "I have no hatred of homosexuals," he said. The court was told how Nilsen had agreed to co-operate fully with the police from the beginning of the investigation. Mr Green told the court how three bodies had been found at Cranley Gardens, one in a wardrobe and one in a tea-chest. Other remains were carved up and flushed down the toilet. Eight bodies, at least, had been found at the accused's former home in Melrose Avenue. Nilsen said he had killed 15 or 16 men and tried to kill about another seven. He denied the six charges of murder and two of attempted murder, but the prosecution said these charges represented only some of the attacks. Mr Green said the defence would "raise the case of diminished responsibility" because of Nilsen's mental state, but what the jury had to decide was whether it was murder or manslaughter. The jury heard how Nilsen had learned certain butchering skills in the Catering Corps, which he put to use after some of the killings. Details were given to the court about how 12 victims were killed at Melrose Avenue. Nilsen hid the body of his first victim, an Irishman, under floorboards, but later burned it in the back garden. Ken Ockenden was his second victim. Victims 10, 11 and 12 remained unidentified; Malcolm Barlow was victim number 13. The death of John Howlett was described by the prosecution as "possibly the most chilling of all". Nilsen strangled him with an upholstery strap, then held his head under water in the bath for four or five minutes. He had to get rid of the body quickly as a friend was coming to stay the following night, so he dismembered John in the bath and flushed the man's flesh and organs down the toilet. Nilsen said: "This proved to be a slow process so I decided to boil some of it, including the head. I put all the large bones out with the rubbish and other pieces into the tea chest." One survivor who awoke to find himself bound by Nilsen managed to convince the killer to let him go. He immediately went to the police, but they were convinced by Nilsen that he and Douglas Stewart had had a lovers' quarrel.

Nilsen pleaded "Not guilty" to all the charges put to him in court. Four warders flanked him and the public gallery was full. At this point, the jury were asked to survey a number of photographs, which Mr Green assured them were not "stomach-churning".

Carl Stotter told the Old Bailey jury on 25th October how he realized that the man who picked him up was trying to kill him. He went to bed with Nilsen and later awoke to find something around his neck. He passed out as the pressure was applied, and when he awoke he heard running water. He remembered being carried and placed in the bath and then being pushed under over and over again. But Nilsen didn't kill the young man, and he awoke to find Bleep licking his face. He managed to leave the house.

Nilsen wrote a number of letters to Detective Chief Inspector Peter Jay following his arrest. In one of them he said: "I think I have sufficient principle and morality to know where the buck must come to rest. The evil was short-lived and cannot live for long outside. Now I have slain my own dragon as surely as the Press will slay me. We are all lying in the gutter – but some of us are winking at the stars." In another letter he said: "I guess that I may be a creative psychopath who when in a loss of rationality situation lapses temporarily into a destructive psychopath, a condition induced by rapid and heavy ingestion of alcohol." The letter continued: "There is no disputing that I am a violent killer under certain circumstances. The victim is the dirty platter after the feast and the washing up is a clinically ordinary task."

Nilsen also told police how children gathered around a bonfire of his burning victims. He described how he burnt the contents of suitcases and carrier bags containing the victims' heads in the garden of his house in Melrose Avenue, and that children came along and prodded the blaze with sticks as he placed old tyres on the fire to mask the smell of burning flesh. He told detectives: "The fire burned extraordinarily fiercely. There were spurts, bangs, crackles and hisses. This I took for fat from the bodies burning." Later he was said to have spotted pieces of skull on the ashes. "I took the garden roller and rolled over the site several times."

Nilsen told Mr Chambers that only people who needed him became victims. Meanwhile, the court heard how he had boiled a victim's head to make disposal easier. A large aluminium cooking pot was held up for the jury to inspect. Nilsen's counsel Ivan Lawrence, QC, said that his client would not go into the witness box. "There will be no more sickening evidence," he said.

It transpired that Nilsen considered himself the "murderer of the century", according to psychiatrist Dr Patrick Gallwey. He is "very close to insanity" but has a "tenacious quality that stops him going mad," the psychiatrist added. "Lots of the time he likes to show off … I don't think he can be relied on to tell the truth in his statement to the police. Many of these are aimed at impressing, some are plain lies." The prosecution's psychiatrist Dr Paul Bowden said: "Nilsen has no mental disease."

The jury were sent out to reach a verdict on 3rd November 1983. Closing for the defence the day before, Ivan Lawrence, QC, said the court had heard dreadful things over the years, "but nothing so bad as in this case". He claimed that Nilsen wasn't insane, but he wasn't normal either.

Nilsen found vulnerable men in "gay pubs", and persuaded them to accompany him home. There he sat them in front of the television and while they watched films or chatted he plied them with spirits. When they dozed off he strangled them. He then used his butchery skills to decapitate and dismember them. Whether he ever ate the body parts of his victims is still unclear, but many strongly believed that Nilsen took his sexual gratification far further than sexual contact and murder.

At first the jury failed to agree whether the self-confessed killer was guilty of murder or manslaughter. However, he was eventually sentenced to life, with a recommendation that he served 25 years. He was found guilty of murdering the six men and dismembering them, and the Old Bailey trial heard how he had probably killed many more.

The following month, Nilsen refused to divulge the name of the inmate who had slashed him with a razor in the exercise yard at Wormwood Scrubs; but Albert Moffat admitted to making the assault. In 1984, inmate Michael Wright (26) said that prisoners risked their lives by taking on a murderer in jail. "Lifers have nothing to lose by killing again," he said. "You don't even look at prisoners like Nilsen because it's seen as a challenge. You just turn away." Moffat was charged with wounding Nilsen, but said he attacked the killer in self-defence.

Towards the end of June 1984, Moffat walked free, having been serving a 13-month sentence for theft. He was due for release, but was held in custody for his four-day trial. As he left the court he said: "I don't regret what I did ... He had 89 stitches, and I wish it had been 189. The man is disgusting." The jury took two hours and 40 minutes to clear Moffat, from Glasgow, of causing grievous bodily harm and wounding Nilsen. They believed his story that Nilsen had made sexual advances towards him. Moffat said he carried a razor blade for protection, and had struck out in self-defence after Nilsen lunged at him in the prison yard, the jury heard. He continued: "There should be an inquiry into how Nilsen was allowed to get close to young men like me. If he approached me in the same way again

I would have no hesitation in doing the same again. I am glad I caused him misery. He committed six murders without any remorse so I had no remorse either. The man is clearly insane and should never be released."

The following year, Nilsen faced a disciplinary hearing after allegedly assaulting a prison officer. In January 1988 he lost his privileges and was given solitary confinement for attacking a warder at Wakefield jail.

In November 1991 it was announced that BBC bosses were to screen a shock documentary about the serial killer which was to include "grisly sketches" from his "diary of death". He drew his victims as they lay trussed and bleeding in his seedy flat. The BBC2 documentary *Monochrome Man* was also going to include clips from videos the killer made. In one, a drunken Nilsen was seen ranting in the kitchen, while in another he was seen cavorting with a boyfriend who left him before the killings began. An actor also demonstrated how Nilsen daubed himself with make-up to resemble a corpse. The 50-minute programme was based on Brian Masters' best-selling study of Nilsen, *Killing for Company*. Series editor Nigel Williams admitted some scenes were "deeply disturbing", but he said: "Nilsen's drawings shed light on his obsession with death. It is essential we try to understand how such atrocities could happen."

The following year, one of Nilsen's former lovers died in a bizarre glue-sniffing experiment. David Gallichan (36), who had lived with Nilsen for 18-months, was found dead with his head in a plastic bag. Inside was a tin of glue. It was thought that Nilsen began killing after

Gallichan ditched him. The coroner recorded an open verdict.

Like a number of other homes up and down the country that formerly belonged to murderers, Nilsen's home had a reputation. While Fred and Rosemary West's house at 25 Cromwell Street in Gloucester was demolished out of respect for the victims they brutally killed in their home, Nilsen's former home in Cranley Gardens was turned from bedsits into four flats. Jane and Peter Macklin bought the basement flat, unperturbed by the house's grisly history. They decided to move out in 1992, but it took two years for a firm offer to be made on their property. The couple claimed it had little to do with its macabre past, and more because it was a basement flat that didn't catch the sun – and there was a recession at the time. However, they did admit that one buyer pulled out at the last minute when his lawyer told him about Nilsen: "People have found it eerie to be in the same place where something like that happened." People driving past were known to slow down to take a closer look at the building, and no. 23 was included in the cab drivers' local knowledge. The woman said to be interested in the flat wasn't bothered at all that Nilsen had once lived on the floors above.

Later that same year, in June 1994, the *Mirror* stated that Nilsen wanted Harrison Ford to play him in a film because he reckoned they looked identical. He had even offered to write the soundtrack to *Killing for Company*, but producer Clive Evans, who was approached by the killer via a third party, vowed: "If he thinks he can influence the film in any way he's mad – and we certainly won't be using his music." Nilsen's bid for "stardom" continued in 1995 when he made a macabre appearance on Channel 4's *The Word*. He sent the late-night show a tape of songs he recorded in his cell in Whitemoor jail, and the programme made a creepy video featuring news footage of Nilsen to accompany the tape. The songs, composed on a mini-electronic organ, include him chanting "It's mating time" over and over again. Tory MP Harry Greenaway slammed the stunt, saying: "It's a disgrace and irresponsible," but a spokesman for *The Word* said: "there is no intention to shock".

In a Home Office study in April 1995 Nilsen was shown porn videos and 250 photographs – including rape scenes and even stills of naked children. He told reporters: "I should sue them. It was most odd. But even in my gay life I tended to be attracted exclusively to effeminate males. What attracted me to them was the feminine signals they gave off. I was never attracted to big butch gay men." The experiment was intended to give psychologists an insight into the minds of sex offenders, and Nilsen's sexual responses were monitored. Horrified prison officers planned to protest to Home Secretary Michael Howard about the "shocking" tests, and John Bartell, chairman of the Prison Officers Association, said: "I really don't understand how you can carry out these experiments on prisoners who, by any definition, will not see the light of day again." Nilsen had already been told that he would never be freed. In an interview from jail, he described the weird tests: "They've got this device whereby you are wired up by a ring on your penis which is wired to a monitor which also records your pulse rate, brain activity, how much you sweat, etc. You sit in a chair for about one and a half hours and you view pictures and active scenarios on video whereby you are aroused.

"I was doing this for the chief psychologist of Albany jail on the Isle of Wight where I used to be held … I was quite happy to do it. A lot of people don't want to expose themselves to any kind of tests of a sexual nature. People never want to reveal the true nature of their sexuality. They want their fantasies to stay secret, but I have come to terms with mine a long time ago." Nilsen didn't react at all to pictures of naked men, but reacted to those of naked women. He said: "They accused me of being a closet heterosexual, of putting on a gay mantle for psychological reasons going back to my childhood, i.e. fear of my mother or whatever."

A sex-crimes expert admitted that the tests carried out on Nilsen were controversial. The experiments – known as penile plethysmography – had a big question mark hanging over their reliability. Ray Wyre said: "It can only be used as a guide. It is not totally accurate. We do not use it as evidence in court or to decide whether a sex offender should be released or not." Mr Wyre was the expert who helped police profile evil child-killer Robert Black, who was jailed in 1994 for the murders of Sarah Harper, Caroline Hogg and Susan Maxwell.

Nilsen had performed some strange rituals with the corpses of the men he killed. In some cases he had bathed and dressed them, and he also lay alongside them in his bed. He was accused of showing little remorse for his crimes, but he claimed that society had branded him a monster. He said: "How can a monster show human emotions like sorrow? Perhaps if I was treated like a human I would."

Later in April 1995, Nilsen admitted that his killing spree was triggered by his "murder" of a litter of unwanted puppies. He told how he had smothered his first human victim, a lover, while in a "drunken grip of fantasy". Following the death of his 10-year-old budgie Hamish in his cell, he wrote a 21-page "analysis" of himself which he called *The Psychograph*. The study ended with the description of the first murder at his flat in Melrose Avenue in 1978, which gave a chilling insight into his warped mind: he wrote that he first killed to ensure that his "dream mate would stay with him forever". The identity of the 16-year-old victim was still a mystery. Nilsen wrote in the third person: "He spent Christmas alone. In the solitude, he sat holding his dog as blank incomprehension unfolded into the next glass of Bacardi and Coke. Inside a drunken grip of fantasy he drifted into the local 'roughhouse' pub on New Year's Eve and there, inside the land of false smiles, stood the boy of his dreams. There followed a blurred affinity of union. They lay naked and entwined in the warm fur of secure thoughts into the early hours of New Year's Day. He wanted it to go into eternity. He was loved and warm and safe from the long, cold night.

"As threatening dawn approached, he knew that this lovely nameless figure beside him would leave as others had always left him. He was seized by a sudden panic, and gripped by an irresistible effort to ensure that his dream mate would stay with him forever. In the desperate heat of 30 years of stumbling frustration, he stopped the youth awakening. By almost instinctive superpower energy he smothered the boy into a permanent passivity. His maladjusted psychograph had rendered one man into a lifeless prop and himself into a killer of men."

Nilsen created an oil painting he called *Bacardi Sunrise* in 1995, which provided a haunting reminder of his savage crimes. The painting featured a rising sun, a handprint in blood and a magazine picture of a naked man holding his head in his hands. A pink triangle represented the strangler's sexuality. The fact that the naked man was painted inside a red cocoon showed that he desperately wanted to hide his shame, according to Dr Terri Apter, a psychologist and Cambridge University lecturer.

By 1998, Nilsen had sparked a bizarre bidding war among publishers who were eager to buy his "vile" autobiography. He wanted a £100,000 advance for the book which contained a graphic account of his slaughter – and three leading publishers were keen to get their hands on the manuscript, smuggled out of Whitemoor jail in Cambridgeshire. But police and victim support groups said he should not be allowed to profit from his terrible crimes, and the 453-page autobiography was branded as "too evil" to go on sale. Labour MP Claire Ward said: "This sort of book should never see the light of day. It's about making money out of crime." Nilsen was described as being incapable of seeing his victims as real people who had died at his hands, and his book had the same cold, detached, style. In it, he claimed he had not enjoyed the killing. He blamed his loveless childhood in Scotland, which he claimed left him with a craving to be looked after. He even claimed "outrageously" that anyone who grew up in the same way might have killed. Nilsen wrote that because he could not drive, cutting up the bodies was the only way he could dispose of them. He described how he had to steel himself for the task, got very drunk beforehand, and was violently sick each time. He also said that the medical student who found the first bag he dumped had been right – the remains were human. His bloody fingerprints were all over the bag, but it was subsequently destroyed by police when they thought the bag contained butchered entrails. This delayed Nilsen's capture by 18 months. David Allison, of the group OutRage, said: "This book seems tasteless, to say the least. It would be distressing to the family and friends of Nilsen's victims."

In December 2003, it was announced that Nilsen had lost a High Court bid for the right to sell his story. *Nilsen: A History of a Drowning Man*, which the killer claimed was his right to "freedom of expression", was deemed by Mr Justice Maurice Kay as inappropriate, and his request for a judicial review of the governor's decision to refuse him access to the draft was thrown out of court. The judge said that Nilsen's crimes were "as grave and depraved as it is possible to imagine".

In 2005, the *Mirror* claimed that Nilsen was high on drink and drugs at Full Sutton jail in Yorkshire, to which he had been transferred. He bragged of prison-brewed booze and cannabis sessions in the safety of his maximum security cell, while violent vendettas raged among the prison population. He claimed that as soon as one cache of booze was discovered by the "screws" another was already on the brew, and that deaths and murders in the prison were rife. The prison did not deny the claims. However, Norman Brennan, director of the Victims of Crime Trust, which represents the families of murder victims, said: "It is outrageous that this should be going on in Full Sutton. But we are not surprised. This is how a lot of murderers spend their time inside. I believe a blind eye is taken in prisons to drink and drug-taking. The prison service don't run our prisons any more. Certain groups of criminals do."

Nilsen's first victim was identified in November 2006 as runaway Stephen Holmes, who had vanished from his London home in 1978. It had taken 28 years for him to be named.

Some claim that Nilsen's alleged cannibalism is the only part of his crimes for which he felt guilty. According to some sources, it was the only part of the case which he felt awkward talking about.

Cannibal at Large
(1985)

A Japanese man who murdered and ate a girlfriend in 1981 was freed in September 1985 from a secure psychiatric hospital in Tokyo because doctors said there was "nothing wrong with him". In fact, Issei Sagawa (52) was a minor celebrity in his home country. He had written eight books, starred in porn films and became a restaurant reviewer. But in June 1981, while living in Paris, he invited a Dutch student to his apartment, shot her in the head and cut into her with a knife. "Finally I take the big knife and push," he said of the incident. He used an electric carving knife to remove some of her flesh and then ate it. Sagawa was arrested, but a judge said he was unfit to stand trial. He was committed to an institution, where the media treated him like a celebrity. After he was freed he changed his name and moved to a flat close to his wealthy parents.

Tsutomu Miyazaki
(1988)

Born prematurely with deformed hands, Tsutomu Miyazaki suffered a great deal of abuse as a child. Even his own family in Japan found him repulsive. He turned to hardcore pornography, anime and horror films, which led, between 1988 and 1989, to the mutilation and murder of four small girls aged four to seven. He sexually molested the corpses of his victims.

Dubbed "Dracula" and "Otaku Murderer", Miyazaki drank the blood of one of his young victims and ate her limbs. He was a random predator who took delight in terrorizing the families of his victims – often sending them letters which outlined the murders in graphic detail. His first victim, Mari Konno, was just five years old. Her body was allowed to decompose before Miyazaki chopped off her hands and feet, which he kept in a cupboard until his arrest. The little girl's bones were burned and then ground into a "powder" before they were posted to her family in a box.

Miyazaki was caught when a little girl he lured to a park before sexually abusing her was confronted by her father – who had been alerted to the attack by his other little girl. Although Miyazaki fled the scene, when he returned to collect his vehicle, police were waiting for him, and he was arrested. He was convicted, sentenced to death and faced the gallows in June 2008. As is the case for a number of other convicted cannibals, the details surrounding his crimes are not available in the public domain.

Arthur Shawcross
(1990)

On 5th January 1990, Arthur Shawcross (44) was charged on suspicion of strangling up to 17 women in Rochester, New York. Shawcross liked to be known as the "real-life Hannibal Lecter". In 1991 he was told he would spend the rest of his life behind bars. The convicted rapist and child killer had served 15 years of a 25-year sentence when he was paroled in 1987. And he killed again.

Nine of Shawcross' victims were sex workers, who were strangled or hit on the head. He mutilated the bodies, and in two cases ate the woman's sexual organs. Psychologists were still arguing in 2001 whether Shawcross had been abused by his mother as a child. He, however, blamed Vietnam for turning him into a monster. "I was trained to kill," he said. "I was not trained to stop. That bothers me."

Jeffrey Dahmer

(1991)

Horrified cops found three human skulls in a fridge when they burst into Jeffrey Dahmer's apartment. More bones were scattered over a stinking carpet in the bedroom – next to a huge barrel of acid. Factory worker Dahmer (31) was arrested on suspicion of murdering at least 12 gay men. Police in Milwaukee, Wisconsin, believed he copied British serial killer Dennis Nilsen. Wisconsin police lieutenant David Vahl said: "We believe Dahmer used the acid to remove flesh from the bones that were strewn around the blood-stained carpet. It was a scene out of hell."

Dubbed the "real-life *Silence of the Lambs* killer", Dahmer confessed to butchering 17 men. Police believed the blond "madman" ate many of his victims while they were still alive – and the killer appeared in court accused of four murders, with more death charges expected to follow. As the unshaven murderer was making his brief appearance before the US judge, more grisly details of his "horrible life" were revealed by his stepmother, Shari. She told how her husband once found bones in a massive vat at an apartment where his son often slept. "We smelt a harsh odour coming from the basement flat," she said. "His father Lionel investigated and found bones and residue in a huge vat. He couldn't tell if they were human or animal. Jeffrey said it was an animal he had found. Even when he was quite young he liked to use acid to scrape the meat off dead animals." Shari also told how Dahmer often took men to the flat in his grandmother's house. "One time he was down there with a man when his granny opened the door. She could see only his bare chest. He warned her: 'You don't want to come down here.' She thought they were naked so she didn't go down."

Police found severed heads, torsos, boxes of body parts and photos and videos of tortured victims in Dahmer's apartment. The killer was arrested after an intended victim escaped and was found dazed in the street, still wearing handcuffs. It was on 22nd July 1991 that two Milwaukee police officers stopped Tracy Edwards, whom they found wandering around at midnight. He said he had escaped from a "weird dude" who had handcuffed him and threatened him with a knife. They drove to Dahmer's home.

Two months earlier, police had visited Dahmer after being called to a scene in the streets outside his apartment. The murderer's "19-year-old lover", Konerak, was found drunk and running around naked. Witnesses recalled that they thought the naked man was just a boy – they also stressed to police that they thought he was terrified. However, officers believing the "man" was drunk listened to Dahmer's version of events, and were convinced they had stumbled on nothing more than a lover's quarrel.

The *Mirror* also reported that the confessed cannibal was suspected of killing five women in Germany. The women had been murdered and their bodies mutilated more than 10 years previously, near an airbase where Dahmer was stationed as a medical orderly while serving with US forces. A public prosecutor in the town of Bad

Kreuznach told a German newspaper: "We have a burning interest in Dahmer. We are checking to see if he could be the killer." He said there were similarities with the murders in America, even though all the German victims were women.

Meanwhile, Tracy Edwards said: "It was as if I was confronting Satan himself." Edwards (32) had been befriended by Dahmer and lured to the mass-murderer's slaughterhouse. He is thought to have been the only survivor of Dahmer's bloodlust. As Edwards poured out his horrifying story, it was revealed that a police blunder had allowed Dahmer to add a 14-year-old boy to his gruesome list of victims. Like Tracy Edwards, Konerak Sinthasomphone had managed to escape the basement apartment. He was lured there on the way to soccer practice, and passed out shortly after accepting one of Dahmer's lethal sleeping cocktails. He was raped, then left alone as Dahmer went out to buy beer. Recovering consciousness, the boy fled naked out of the flat with blood running down his legs. Two women saw Dahmer catch up with him in the street and, realizing the boy was in trouble, telephoned the police. Within minutes a fire engine and three patrol cars arrived. In his sly, manipulative way, Dahmer persuaded police that the boy was his 19-year-old lover and they had been quarrelling. He told them his lover was drunk, and that he was sorry for wasting their time. Konerak's broken English and his drugged state made it impossible for him to argue. Police accompanied them as Dahmer practically carried the boy back to the flat. Less than an hour later, the boy was dead, strangled before Dahmer had sex with the corpse. He took photographs of his victim, dismembered him and kept Konerak's skull. The remains were among those found in Dahmer's flat. Police were aware at the time that the lad had been reported missing by his anguished parents – and they also knew that the boy's 13-year-old brother had been sexually assaulted by Dahmer in 1988; he lived just one street away from the killer. Three officers were suspended, and police chief Philip Arreola said: "I have ordered an immediate investigation. I send my deepest apologies to the family of the victim." The police had failed to notice the bad smell coming from the basement apartment when they returned Konerak to Dahmer: in the bedroom was the three-day-old rotting corpse of another victim, Tony Hughes.

Dahmer had been killing for 10 years by the time police arrested him. Police believed that he could have been responsible for many more deaths than the 17 he had confessed to. Tracy Edwards said: "I met Dahmer at a shopping mall. He seemed a friendly guy and I agreed to drop by for a beer." When they arrived at Dahmer's apartment Edwards sat down. Moments later, Dahmer crept up behind him and handcuffed him. "He then came at me, threatening me with a knife," Edwards said. Still manacled, he leapt up, dashed from the building and was thankful that the police patrol car spotted him. He added: "I met the Devil face to face and escaped. He underestimated me. God sent me there to take care of the situation. I feel so grateful to be alive."

Dahmer admitted eating his victims' flesh, but Tracy Edwards would not say if he saw any human remains in the killer's flat. However, he did recall the putrid stench. Court papers released on

26th July 1991 detailed the horrific murder of one of the 11 men who were killed at the apartment. Dahmer said he picked up Oliver Lacey (35) in a gay bar, then took him home and offered him $50 to pose for nude photographs. The pair then stripped and Lacey was handed a drugged drink. He was strangled. Dahmer told police he sliced up the body and kept the heart in the freezer "to eat later". His father told reporters: "There's no doubt he's insane. I feel like I should wake up any moment. I don't think I knew him at all."

Another of his son's victims was 25-year-old Joseph Bradehoft. He came from Illinois, and his case was one of a number of disappearances being probed in other American states. Police in Germany had also opened a number of unsolved murder cases.

The three officers who believed Dahmer when he said he had had a lover's tiff with the 14-year-old boy failed to notice the body of Tony Hughes lying in the bedroom. They also missed the gruesome photos of nude and tortured victims strewn around the floors and tables. And police radio traffic tapes revealed the three officers joked about getting deloused after they left the "neat" but "smelly" apartment.

In August 1991, it was claimed that Dahmer was being sued for up to £3.6 billion by the families of three of his alleged victims. Each group of relatives was seeking damages of almost £1.2 billion if Dahmer or any of his family sold their story about the case for use in books or films. By this time, police knew he'd killed another 14-year-old boy, while another victim was identified as 19-year-old Stephen Hicks, whom Dahmer had picked up hitchhiking. He was killed at Dahmer's childhood home in Ohio. All the other American victims were thought to have died in Milwaukee.

The *Mirror* wrote on 13th January 1992: "The long corridor leading to the small seedy flat quickly fills you with a sense of unease. It is quiet. Empty. The people who once lived on the second floor of this apartment block have fled.

"In daylight, the fluorescent lights remain on, bathing the area in an unearthly pallor. Then there is the smell. The sickly odour lingering around the door of Flat 213 that not even the strongest disinfectant can smother. Last July, when this door was thrown open, it revealed some of the most hideous sights ever recorded in America's criminal history. The spectacle that awaited Milwaukee's murder squad was so horrendous officers needed counselling afterwards.

"What they found in 213 Oxford Apartments was nothing less than a human abattoir. As the stench of the flat forced police to don masks, the occupant, 31-year-old homosexual Jeffrey Dahmer, was being led away in handcuffs, whimpering in soft, cat-like miaow sounds. The scenario that followed would inevitably be compared with the film *The Silence of the Lambs*.

"Dahmer's friendless life in Milwaukee, Wisconsin, enabled him to spend days undisturbed, sawing bones and preparing flesh-eating chemicals. In his kitchen stood a 57-gallon barrel of acid full of torsos, limbs and hands. On the shelves of his fridge sat four male heads. There was no food. Only a human heart. Dahmer told police: 'I was keeping it so I could eat it later.' Seven painted skulls sat trophy-like on shelves around the rest of the two-roomed flat. On the walls were more than a hundred photos showing mutilated men.

The door of 213 is now locked and barred, its interior sealed forever.

"Not unlike the mind of Jeffrey Dahmer. Blond, bland, blue-eyed Jeffrey sits in his cell in Milwaukee County Jail, staring into space, waiting for his trial on January 27, when he will plead guilty due to insanity. Depressed and withdrawn, Dahmer is being kept on constant suicide watch. He is charged with the murder of 15 men, although he has confessed to killing 17 and to committing acts of cannibalism. Gerald Boyle, the top lawyer hired by Dahmer's father, first met him in 1988 when he was charged with child molesting. Boyle says: 'No-one suspected then that he had already killed people. He seemed to me to be someone who wanted to be rehabilitated. My problem now is making sure I see him most days in order to keep him mentally occupied. If total withdrawal sets in then he could disintegrate.' As to how the elder of two sons from a prosperous middle-class background began his descent into hell, no-one knows.

"Lionel Dahmer, a research chemist, divorced Jeffrey's mother Joyce in 1978. Soon afterwards he married Shari Jordan. From their home in Ohio, Shari spoke to me of the horror befalling the Dahmer family and of her husband Lionel's anguish. 'The pain for my husband is dreadful. But I knew when I first met Jeff that there was no hope of him becoming one of life's achievers,' says the blond businesswoman. 'He was 18 then, practically an alcoholic, and beyond my help, so I concentrated on the younger son, David. We are all searching for answers,' she said. 'We talk to Jeff during our visits and he doesn't have any clues either. None of us know why, out of two children with a similar upbringing, one should become a killer.'

"Dahmer's days at Richfield High School, Ohio offer some clues. Classmate Marth Schmidt remembers him as 'a lost, tortured soul I felt sad for. I used to see him drinking Scotch, and I'd ask him why he was doing that. He'd just say: "It's my medicine."'"

Dahmer's idea of fun was to impersonate disabled people, and he rolled around the floor in class, behaving in a way he thought was outrageous. To his classmates, he was just attention-seeking, goofy and pathetic. Neighbour Eric Tyson said that Dahmer kept chipmunk and squirrel skeletons in a shed: "People recall him impaling animals like frogs and cats." Aberrant behaviour like this seemed to imply a deeply disturbed child who felt unloved. A school official suggested that Dahmer's feelings of neglect began as early as six years old, when his brother David was born. His mother Joyce was ill, and shortly afterwards the marriage became so hopeless that she and her husband had separate bedrooms. Friends talked of how Dahmer's father strung up bells outside his room to warn him of Joyce's arrival. Years later, Dahmer confided to a probation officer: "If I could change anything in my childhood, it would be the way my parents behaved towards each other." The *Mirror* continued: "It was all too much for Jeffrey to handle. He needed an escape route." Police were told he had been lost in a fantasy world since childhood and that alcohol aided his escape. In that private place he created, Dahmer was king. Everybody paid attention to him. Nobody laughed at him, or walked away when he came into a room. He was popular, clever, charming and powerful. "And very soon Jeffrey was going to enact some of those powerful feelings he felt when he was in his private place."

When Jeffrey's parents divorced, his mother moved away with his brother, and his father left to marry Shari. Dahmer felt more abandoned than ever. He was 18, home alone, waiting to begin life at Ohio State University, when one day while out driving he spotted a young blond man trying to hitch a ride. He invited Stephen Hicks home. They drank beer, played music and then Stephen made a terrible mistake – he said he had to leave. Dahmer took a dumb-bell and smashed Stephen's skull into a bloodied pulp. He then hauled the body outside, and with the long hunting knife he had used on animals sliced up Stephen's body and buried his remains in nearby woods. Perhaps the killer shocked himself, because it would be another nine years before he killed again. In the meantime, he was found guilty of child molestation and given five years' probation.

Dahmer lasted just one term at university before enlisting for six years in the US Army, but he was discharged after three for excessive drinking. He drifted around Florida before returning to Milwaukee to live with his grandmother, Catherine Dahmer. There he found a job draining blood in the Milwaukee Blood Bank. While living in his basement flat, he began to invite round men he fancied for beers. He found them by stalking the shadowy streets of the city, or hanging round the Greyhound bus stop. The initial request must have seemed harmless. "Would you like to come back with me, have a beer, watch videos?" He was a "nice"-looking guy so victims were easily seduced. What his grandmother didn't know was that three of the men Jeffrey brought home never left. They were killed, dismembered and then buried in the grounds around her house. She suspected nothing. "Jeffrey was a helpful boy, loving and thoughtful enough to help with tasks like mowing the lawn," said the *Mirror*.

Dahmer's next job was labouring at the Ambrosia Chocolate Company, which lasted six years until he was fired for erratic timekeeping, a week before his arrest. A social outcast from his well-placed family, he was a continual source of worry to them.

"I know," said Shari, "but since his arrest, Jeff has told me that nothing more could have been done for him. He doesn't know why he did those terrible things. He told me if he'd been caught after the first murder in 1978, it would have been a blessing. I cannot describe to you what a nightmare this has been. All I will say is every parent should realize that there, but for the grace of God, go I."

Lionel Dahmer seemed as bewildered as his wife, but the psychological clues had always been there. Dahmer, the eternal outsider incapable of forming a relationship, had all the classic traits of a serial killer. The *Mirror* reported that it seemed unfair to blame Dahmer's parents – yet society would normally look to family background. His father and stepmother were anguished about what he had done. While his relationship with his mother seemed as though it was complicated and distant, his father had been loving, gentle and supportive.

Dahmer had given up his affluent suburban life for the cheap, soulless apartment block on the outskirts of Milwaukee. Friendless and aimless, he whiled away his social hours in his flat drinking, listening to Black Sabbath and watching violent videos. He frequented gay bars, and Club 219 became one of his haunts. Barman Terry Scott's description of him was typical. "He almost blended in to the point he wasn't there. He never looked as though he was having a good time. I don't think he picked anyone up here. I don't remember him talking to anyone, and this is a friendly place." Evan Zeepos, Dahmer's boss at Ambrosia, said: "He worked here for six years as part of a team moving bulk, and he was basically a satisfactory employee. He was fired because of attendance problems. He wasn't friends with anyone. I think there was only one person he spoke to in the works changing room. And when I say speak, I mean 'Hi' or 'Goodbye'. He was a loner ... and because he was so distant, we had no idea of the tragedy unfolding."

The manager of Dahmer's apartment block, Sopa Princewill, also spoke of him as someone you wouldn't normally notice, except that he was the only white guy on the block. "There was a terrible smell coming from his flat. Everybody was complaining. When I went up to inquire, Dahmer said he had been too busy to notice that the freezer had broken down and all his meat had gone off. I noticed handcuffs and surgical masks lying around, and a big barrel in the kitchen. He said it was acid for the roaches. I believed him."

Dahmer lived in an area with "the have-nots" and the "isolated social misfits" who were generally unemployed, wrestling with drug problems. "People," the *Mirror* wrote, "the American dream had passed by." Dahmer's former next-door neighbour, Sheila White, asked angrily: "How come all those men were going in there and never coming out? Why didn't the police do something? Was it because us black folk ain't worth bothering about?" It would have been hard to find a Milwaukee police officer who would admit to such feelings, but how else could anyone explain the death of Konerak at the age of 14?

Dahmer's urge to kill had become an insatiable frenzy by the time of Konerak's death in May 1991, and between then and July four more men were butchered. Mr Edwards would have been Dahmer's fifth victim had he not escaped.

The carnage, the shame and the shock culminated in a trial that would decide the question of Dahmer's sanity. A psychiatrist who had studied other serial killers as well as Dahmer said: "A lot of people have a tough childhood, but it doesn't turn them into mass murderers. When something like Dahmer happens, you search for reasons, and all I can come up with is a belief in the forces of good and evil. I think that Dahmer was just born the way he was. Evil. There is no one to blame, no one to answer for what happened, or for what he became. Let us just say that maybe some people should never have been born. They are one of nature's mistakes."

Dahmer was pronounced sane by the jury at his three-week trial in Milwaukee and jailed for life 15 times on 17th February 1992; he still faced trial in Ohio for his first murder 14 years previously. He was to receive mandatory life terms and was to be sent to Wisconsin's newest top security prison at Portage. Victim Eddie Smith's sister, Carolyn (37), said she was "delighted" by the verdict. Dahmer made a "sick threat" when he said that he would murder more victims and cannibalize them if he were ever set free. He was given 999 years (although this was increased later) for killing his victims over a 13-year period.

Dahmer told a US television show, *Inside Edition*, that he still had "terrible compulsions" to kill. He said that killing and eating the young men he lured to his apartment was the only satisfaction he gained in his whole warped life. He said that the film *Exorcist III* made him feel good – because he thought he was more evil than the film's characters. And he told how he took the mummified head of a victim to work at Ambrosia so he could stare at it during his lunch break. He also told the programme that he liked to eat the heart of his victims because he felt that it made them part of him.

On 28th November 1994, the world was rid of "monster" Jeffrey Dahmer. He was bludgeoned to death with a broom handle in a jail bathroom. He had already survived another murder bid, when an inmate lunged for his throat with a razor, and a survived suicide attempt, but it was claimed that prison guards might have turned a blind eye to the murder of the cannibal serial killer. Two guards should have been watching the murderer, who was under a constant threat of death, but they were both missing when a fellow prisoner attacked Dahmer while he cleaned a staff bathroom at the jail in Portage. Sources within the jail indicated that the guards might have deliberately left him alone: they would have known that vengeance would be exacted on the 17-times killer. Wife-killer Jesse Andrews was also badly injured in the attack. Officials at the maximum security jail did not reveal the identity of the killer as the newspapers clamoured for the story.

The lawyer Gerald Boyle said: "Dahmer had a death wish but was too cowardly ever to take his own life. He may have put himself in harm's way because he never had the guts to do it himself." The murder came as no surprise. Dahmer had been under sentence of death ever since the jail doors slammed behind him in 1992, and lifers without hope of parole vied for the "honour" of carrying out the hit. An inmate who had sworn for the previous 12 months to kill Dahmer was thought to have carried out the attack. Dahmer had remained an object of loathing in jail because he never seemed to show any genuine remorse for his crimes. In a jailhouse interview in 1994 he said that the terrible compulsions which drove him had never left him. In an interview transcript given exclusively to the *Mirror*, Dahmer told how he planned on setting up a shrine littered with the skulls of his victims surrounded by candles. He was eventually caged for 1,070 years, with no possibility of parole for 930 years.

Following the trial, police revealed how Dahmer had kept body parts in a lobster pot in one of his cupboards along with skulls and fingers. The fridge contained human hamburgers. Dahmer said: "I never killed because I was angry with people. Not because I hated them. It was because I wanted to keep them with me." Dahmer's victims included James Doxtater (15), Richard Guerrero (23), Raymond Smith, aka Ricky Beeks (30), Edward Smith (28), Ernest Miller (23), David Thomas (23), Curtis Straughter (17), Errol Lindsey (19), Matt Turner aka Donald Montrell (21), Jeremiah Weinberger (24), Steven Tuomi, Oliver Lacey (25), Joseph Bradehoft (25), Stephen Hicks (19), Tony Hughes (32) and Konerak Sinthasomphone (14).

Relatives of Dahmer's cannibalized victims were delighted to hear of his death. Rita Isbell, sister of Errol Lindsey, said: "He died the way he deserved to die – like a dog. It was too long in coming, that is my only feeling." John Smith, whose son Edward was dismembered and disposed of in rubbish bags after Dahmer had violated his corpse in 1990, said: "I thought he was the devil on earth and deserved to die. I shall weep no tears for his passing – rather I find it a cause for celebration." The families, who had listened to some of the most gruesome testimony ever offered in a criminal court case, had formed a loose association since Dahmer's conviction. Many of them protested vociferously when they heard that he was seeking to auction household items from his flat, including his fridge. Now that he had been brutally murdered, there was only relief. "There was no place for him on earth," said Mary Reilly, aunt of Matt Turner, who was murdered, his body dissolved in acid. "I will toast his death with a drink," she said.

In his book *A Father's Story*, Lionel Dahmer told how his son had nailed frogs, cats and dogs to trees, locked the skeletons of chipmunks and squirrels in his garden shed and worshipped them, and that he impaled a dog's head on a stick. He once persuaded a playmate to stick his hand into a wasp's nest and then laughed at the child's agony. All the danger signs were there; but Lionel believed his son's demons had gone by the time he reached adulthood. He had actually thought things were getting better just before his son was arrested. He admitted: "I am shocked how little I knew about him. Not just in terms of his crimes but in the number of experiences he managed to hide from me – his abnormal fantasies at the age of 10, homosexuality at 14, alcoholism at 17, murder at 18, lobotomies performed on his victims, having sex with the dead bodies, dismemberment and cannibalism. The list is horrifying. Which is my son – the gentle insecure boy who used to go with me every Saturday morning for a cherry ice cream soda, or the twisted killer that took his place? ... I feel guilty that I didn't do more. I feel a deep sense of shame." Profits from the book were reported to be going to victims' families, but they didn't: they went to Lionel Dahmer. He refused to talk about his son's death unless he received cash offers in excess of £17,500.

On 18th December 1994 shackled lifer Christopher Scarver, who once claimed to be the son of God, briefly appeared in court to be accused of murdering Dahmer and another prisoner, Jesse Anderson, at Portage. Scarver (25) had smashed the serial killer over the head with a steel bar, and told detectives: "I left him gurgling on the floor because God told me to do it." The 20-inch bar had been stolen from the prison gym.

On the orders of a judge, many of the items that Dahmer used during his killing spree were to be auctioned, including the acid bath he used to dispose of victims. The judge wanted the items to be sold in order to raise money for the victims' families. Lots included the hacksaw Dahmer had used to cut up bodies and the power drill he used to bore holes into his drugged victims' foreheads while they were still alive. Pictures of the dead were also to be sold, alongside the cutlery and plates he used for midnight snacks of human flesh.

Dahmer's kettle had contained two hands and a set of genitals at the time of his arrest.

Tracy Edwards appeared on the US chat show *Geraldo*, but then, unable to cope with the trauma of his experience, his life fell apart. He was wanted in 2001 by police in connection with cocaine dealing charges, and was living as a fugitive.

Black Magic in Epping Forest
(1991)

Naked devil-worshippers sacrificed babies and persistently raped two little sisters during black magic orgies in a forest clearing, the Old Bailey heard on 13th November 1991. Prosecuting QC Michael Lawson told how the girls claimed the orgies began with a rabbit's throat being cut and its blood dripping into a chalice, which was then passed around. Then the girls were given another drink tasting like weak orange juice, which one said "made everything echoey". A "gipsy's" memorial stone was covered in black cloth and a candle, stars and horns were placed on it. The adults, some naked and some dressed in black, made a "terrible humming" sound – and chanted names such as Lucifer and Beelzebub as they danced around a bonfire. The QC said: "The eldest girl would be placed on the stone. Gibbard would service her first. Other males would follow, sometimes singly or in combination. At times males would abuse her together. The younger girl would receive similar treatment while lying on the ground." The lawyer added that according to the girls, babies were sometimes placed on the stone after the sex orgies. The sisters claimed that the infants were then slaughtered with a knife, and sometimes they were ordered to dismember the babies' bodies with a bayonet.

Five people faced a total of 20 charges dating back to 1982, including rape and other serious sexual offences. They included the parents of the girls, a 44-year-old caretaker and a woman of 35, and the alleged "king and queen" of the coven – George Gibbard (58) and his 57-year-old lover Rosemary Ridewood. The girls claimed that the coven met every week in Epping Forest in Essex, and that they had endured years of sexual abuse after being taken to the clearing from their East London home.

Other children were said to be at the rituals. Mr Lawson said the girls claimed to have seen jobless Gibbard, of South Woodford, slash the throats of babies. The QC added: "Once a boy of about seven had a noose around his neck tied to a tree and was standing on a stool. The stool was taken away and the boy was pulled down and the rope broke." The sisters' father allegedly dug graves for the bodies, but sometimes he took them home and hid them under the stairs in plastic bags before burning them in a nearby garage. Mr Lawson said: "These slaughters would also take place at the home address. The girls claim that blood would spill and splash but by the following morning there was nothing to be seen."

All the charges were denied, and the QC told the jury it was up to them to decide if the sisters were telling the truth. Police had not turned up anything to support them – and there were no known missing babies. But medical evidence suggested the girls had been abused, and the case continued.

The girl of 10 clutched a pink toy rabbit on 14th November as she told the court how her father often forced her into sex. She said: "I thought it must happen to everyone." The girl and her 14-year-old sister were now much older than when the abuse had begun. The child was back in court the following day, and she wept as she told the court how she was forced to take part in child murders and cannibalism at the satanic ceremonies. Devil worshippers queued to gang rape her as their parents watched, the Old Bailey heard. Giving evidence from behind screens, the child said all the evidence about her abuse was true, but she was not sure whether she had imagined the killings or not. She said that the coven called her "angel of the devil" and that the coven leader sometimes made her hold the knife as he pushed it into helpless children. "My sister had to do it a few times as well," she said. Sometimes he forced her to eat some of the flesh, she told the jury.

The girl said that she and her sister were taken "about three times a week" to naked rituals in the forest, and given drinks which made her feel "dizzy and sexy". She described being ordered to lie on the ground while men sexually abused her. The girl said her mother warned she would be "cut up and hanged" by gypsies if she told what was happening. "I was scared. I believed it – I believed whatever they told me," she said. She eventually told her grandmother. The case continued, but eventually collapsed as nothing was ever proved.

Alexander Spesivtsev

(1991)

In 1991, Alexander Spesivtsev began killing all the children in his local Russian town whom he deemed unfit to live and detrimental to society. The "street kids" he targeted often came from a background similar to his own – abusive and violent. The bodies of his victims were cooked at the home he shared with his mother, Lyudmila. Both mother and son are documented as having eaten the flesh of these child victims. The press dubbed the killer "The Cannibal of Siberia" as the number of missing children grew to 19.

A neighbour called a plumber to the apartment building where Spesivtsev lived after a broken pipe caused continuing problems. The plumber became suspicious when nobody answered the door of the murderer's home and forced his way into the dwelling. He could not have imagined what he would find. When he saw blood covering the walls he immediately called the police, who found a young girl mutilated, but still alive, on the sofa. She gave vital information to police but died shortly afterwards. There was also a decapitated body in the bath and in the kitchen bowls were full of human flesh. Spesivtsev had set his two vicious dogs on two young girls. The young girl in the bathtub hadn't stood a chance. After the dogs killed her in front of Spesivtsev, he cut off her head. He hadn't yet had the time to dismember the rest of her body.

A diary found in the apartment detailed the murders of 19 children, but police believed the number of victims was significantly more. Spesivtsev was ruled insane and committed to a secure hospital. His mother was convicted of being an accomplice and served 13 years in jail. While the case is thought to be one of the worst with regard to cannibalism, documentary evidence suggests that Russia has had the highest number of criminal cannibals in history. Russian police believe that the country has suffered at the hands of more than 500 perpetrators.

John Bunting
(1992)

After a series of events dubbed the Snowtown murders, carried out between August 1992 and May 1999 in South Australia, the remains of eight victims were found in barrels at a rented building. The crimes were traced to a ringleader, John Bunting, who ran a gang that preyed on the vulnerable local residents of Snowtown, stealing their welfare benefits. The gang were intent on targeting paedophiles and homosexuals, and welfare fraud soon turned to murder.

Bunting instructed his gang in all the crimes, and alongside fellow gang member, Robert Wagner, cannibalized David Johnson, one of the men's victims. Another gang member, James Vlassakis, told police how Bunting and Wagner hacked at the victim until his body would fit in the barrel, then took flesh from the victim's right thigh.

They heated the flesh in a frying pan, cooked and ate it. Bunting and Wagner were convicted to life imprisonment following what was one of Australia's most expensive criminal cases. The authorities in Australia remain reluctant to reveal any details of the cannibalism which took place during the murders.

Andrei Chikatilo
(1992)

The real-life "the Cannibal" gave a sinister smile in court as he was found guilty of 52 murders on 14th October 1992. "Evil" grandfather Andrei Chikatilo was known as the Rostov Ripper after slaughtering 21 boys, 14 girls and 17 women in Russia. The 56-year-old monster also ate body parts of his victims. Others were mutilated or raped in his 12-year reign of terror. The former literature teacher was expected to be sentenced on 15th October and shot in the back of the head. His victims' families, who were forced to hear the 330-page verdict, screamed for his blood as the bulging-eyed killer sat in a white metal cage in the courtroom. One woman shouted: "Let me tear him apart with my hands." Relatives had wept when they heard how Chikatilo cut out hearts, stomachs and tongues and gouged out eyes while his victims were still alive.

Chikatilo tried to show he was mad, but psychiatrists said he was sane. He was caught after the biggest manhunt in Soviet history – one littered with blunders. Three other suspects were arrested and one was executed for one of the Ripper's murders. A second suspect killed himself. At one stage Chikatilo was arrested – but was then released and free to kill again.

Ian Warby
(1993)

Madman Ian Warby dreamed of becoming a serial killer like his "hero" Hannibal the Cannibal in *The Silence of the Lambs*. He planned to eat his victims' lips and tongues, sew up their mouths with needle and thread and hammer nails through their kneecaps. In one day, he attacked five people – including a woman in a wheelchair – near his home in Witham, Essex, but he failed to inflict any serious injuries. Defence counsel told the High Court on 7th May 1993 that Warby (26) was a pathetic "emotional cripple". He asked for him to be sent back to a psychiatric hospital, which had released him in 1991. But the prosecution said he was a dangerous psychopath who should be jailed for life. The judge was to sentence Warby after further study of psychiatric reports.

He jailed Warby for life on 11th May 1993 for his "orgy" of hammer and knife attacks. Warby, who called himself The Panther, had to listen as the judge was told that he was actually "weedy".

Peter Bryan

(1993)

In October 1993, Peter Bryan killed Nisha Sheth (20), a shop assistant, in a frenzied hammer attack. He was sent to Rampton Secure Hospital in 1994 after admitting to the unlawful killing.

In February 2004, Bryan was charged with the murder of a man whose body had been found dismembered. Hours before "harmless" Brian Cherry (42) died, Bryan left the secure hospital where he had become a voluntary in-patient. Mr Cherry's flat in East London was a bloody scene of apparent cannibalism, and a brain was being fried in the kitchen. On 19th February, Bryan was remanded in custody and led from court in handcuffs.

Mr Cherry was believed to have had both arms and a leg severed as his flat became a scene of horror that suggested a cannibalistic killing. Bryan had discharged himself from hospital and killed the man in cold blood. Mr Cherry's neighbours in nearby Walthamstow had made desperate 999 calls. Blood was found on the walls and floor of the ground-floor council flat. Neighbour Sharon Perry (25) said: "Brian was so friendly and harmless. He had problems – he was epileptic and always had bruises on his face because he used to fall." His mother had died just weeks before.

Health chiefs had been investigating Bryan's case, and East London and the City Mental Health Trust confirmed that an "in-patient" had been charged with murder. But Bryan had been convincing hospital staff for some time that his mental health had significantly improved and that he no longer posed a danger to anyone.

Bryan (35) was initially sent to Rampton in Nottingham after he killed the shop assistant, but seven years later he was transferred to a less secure unit in North London, where he could come and go as he pleased. He was then moved to an open psychiatric ward in East London. During day leave he killed his friend Brian Cherry. He was then sent to Broadmoor, with a recommendation that he be locked up in the most secure part of the hospital. But he was put in medium security, where he strangled a fellow patient, killer Richard Loudwell. Loudwell (60) was found with a pyjama cord around his neck and serious head injuries. He died two months later.

The string of errors that allowed Bryan to roam free were investigated by three separate inquiries. The first examined the "care and treatment" of Loudwell until his admission to Broadmoor. The second concentrated on the treatment of Bryan and his contact with mental health experts before the killing of Mr Cherry. The third inquiry looked at how Loudwell and Bryan came to be admitted to Broadmoor, and their treatment there – including why nurses cleaned up the blood-stained monster after he attacked Loudwell. Bryan calmly told staff, who also put his bloody clothes in the laundry: "I have harmed myself." A nurse revealed: "He was extremely persuasive." The first report was expected within six months. A Broadmoor spokeswoman said: "We'll be looking very closely at what went wrong and make recommendations. We cannot comment further until the inquiry reports are published." The three-part investigation was one of the biggest ever into mental health services and was expected to cost tens of thousands of pounds. An executive summary was to be published once all three inquiries had reached their final conclusions. Meanwhile, new legislation to give greater protection to the public instead of protecting the rights of patients was to be considered by the Government.

In September 2009, NHS failures were blamed for allowing Bryan to murder two more people after he was freed from hospital. The killer, who was described as schizophrenic, had been released into the community without adequate supervision. The report found that Bryan had been given an inexperienced social worker and a psychiatrist who had never worked with a convicted killer. Tory health spokeswoman Anne Milton said: "This was a complete failure of mental health and social services."

Shockingly, in March 2012, it was revealed that two dangerous patients who hurt themselves opening windows at Broadmoor had won £7,500 in compensation. They were among six of Britain's most notorious killers and rapists at the psychiatric unit who had pocketed £64,000 in payouts in the previous five years. One was granted £10,000 after receiving the wrong medicine and another £4,500 after he was injured being restrained by nurses. The family of murderer Richard Loudwell was given £40,000 in 2009, the largest single payout to an inmate's family, after he was killed by Bryan.

China's Cultural Revolution Hits the Headlines

(1994)

Thousands of victims of China's infamous Cultural Revolution were butchered and eaten, it was revealed on 6th September 1994. Their flesh was served up in government cafeterias, where human corpses were displayed dangling from meat hooks. Some students killed and cooked their teachers in schoolyards. The "grisly" secrets were discovered in classified reports studied by two American authors who were researching their new book, *China Wakes*. The episode of cannibalism was "the biggest in modern times", they said. It occurred during the height of the mass hysteria which swept China in the late 1960s.

Some fanatical young Red Guards, set on a rampage by Communist leader Chairman Mao Tse-tung, followed orders to eat their "class enemies". They willingly became cannibals – motivated by politics, not hunger, says the book. "At some high schools, students butchered and roasted their teachers, feasting on the meat to celebrate triumph over 'counter-revolutionaries'." The first person to strip meat from the body of one school principal was the former girlfriend of the man's son. "She wanted to show she had no sympathy for him and was as 'red' as anybody else," authors Nicholas Kristof and Sheryl WuDunn reported. Hundreds of thousands of people were murdered in the Cultural Revolution. The cannibalism was largely confined to Southern China, and mostly took place during 1967, according to records.

Jason Mitchell
(1995)

"Crazed Jason Mitchell slaughtered his father and a pensioner couple in a horrific rehearsal for cannibal carnage," wrote the *Mirror* on 8th July 1995. He planned to copy *The Silence of the Lambs* movie psycho Hannibal Lecter, who ate his victims. Mitchell's 54-year-old father, Bob, and the two 65-year-olds were "too old to eat"; but schizophrenic Mitchell was preparing to stalk – and devour – younger victims. The tattooed strangler launched his killing spree after being freed early from a psychiatric hospital – and only seven months after being declared fit to live in the community. One psychiatrist described him as "a pleasant young man with no sign of malice". On 7th July 1995, 24-year-old Mitchell was jailed for life for the crimes that shocked the nation.

He sat silently in the dock at Ipswich Crown Court, Suffolk, as the grisly story unfolded. On his face were two sinister tattoos – a devil worship-style cross in the middle of his forehead, and a human skull with a snake slithering through eye sockets. The court heard how Mitchell had struck in the picturesque village of Bramford, Suffolk just before Christmas in 1994. He strangled Arthur and Shirley

Wilson in their bungalow, then throttled his father at his home 200 yards away. Mitchell cut up his father's body and hid the head, arms and legs in the attic. After his arrest, he told police he had wanted to kill his father since he was six years old and had once tried to smother him with a pillow. The prosecutor said: "Later he said he wanted to kill and eat the Wilsons and his father, but did not do it because they were too old.

"The reason he killed the Wilsons was to confirm his ability to kill. He cut up his father as practice for cutting up someone younger who he could eat. He expressed no remorse other than the fact that his arrest ended his ambition to kill again. He was only sorry that he had been caught and couldn't carry out his ambition to kill and eat someone."

The trail of blunders that led to bloodshed began after an Old Bailey judge ordered Mitchell to be detained for life in a secure psychiatric hospital. The young loner from a broken home had left school at 16 and never had a proper job. He drifted into drug-taking and petty crime and already had a string of 13 convictions for burglary and theft when he appeared at the Old Bailey in 1990. Mitchell admitted attacking 70-year-old church cleaner Jim Powell with a baseball bat. He also told police: "I heard voices in my head and they told me to kill the vicar." Doctors diagnosed Mitchell as a paranoid schizophrenic and a danger to the community, but two mental health review tribunals ruled that his condition had improved after treatment. In May 1994, he was granted limited release back into the community. He began his mad rampage on 12th December that year.

Retired stationmaster Arthur Wilson and his wife Shirley were the first to die. Mitchell got into their home through an unlocked garage door and waited for two hours before springing his deadly ambush. The Wilsons were known as local "Good Samaritans". They lived next to the little Methodist church where they worshipped every Sunday and where Shirley played the organ. Arthur often used his car to take villagers to hospital and clinics. Christmas fairy lights twinkled in the front window of the devoted couple's bungalow as the killer lurked inside. He showed no mercy. Both were bound hand and foot; Shirley was strangled with her scarf, her husband with a pair of her tights. Later the killer slipped along the street to cruelly slaughter his own father, and to butcher the body with a hacksaw and knife.

Mitchell's fingerprints were found in the bungalow. The butt of a Red Bank cigarette also linked him to the scene. Police found him sitting in darkness in his father's council house. He denied murder in court, but pleaded guilty to manslaughter on the grounds of diminished responsibility. He was given three life sentences – each for a minimum of 20 years. The judge, Mr Justice Blofeld, called him extremely dangerous and declared: "On the face of it you should not have been released." At Mitchell's original trial the judge had warned: "Any person may be at risk if he suffers a relapse." He was sent to West Park Hospital in Epson for treatment, and then granted permission to move to a hospital – St Clements – in Ipswich, which was closer to his home; here he was allowed some freedom with supervision. Mitchell moved to a halfway house – Linkways – in the grounds of St Clements in February 1994, and was allowed to go out on trips alone. The decision to allow him back into the community in August that year was backed by the then Home Secretary Michael Howard. Later, Mitchell was transferred to Larkhill hostel in Lowestoft, which was run by the charity MIND. He returned to St Clements after four months as a lodger – being allowed to come and go as he pleased – because he didn't get on with other residents. He failed to return to his home on 9th December, three days before the murders.

Arthur and Shirley's daughter told reporters that Mitchell should never have been allowed out from behind bars. "We hope this evil man will never be free to walk the streets again," she said. Jill Benson continued: "Mum and Dad were two active, healthy people who were looking forward to a long and happy retirement. This was snatched from them. Their murder was totally senseless and futile. How could a man like this be allowed to walk free. Someone ... made a grave error of judgment."

Mitchell's sister, Fiona, said she had last seen her brother in April 1994, when he seemed in "good spirits and quite normal". She claimed that his behaviour worsened after St Clements changed his medication, saying: "Nobody in authority picked up on it. I feel they have a lot to answer for." Referring to her "much-loved" father, she added: "I will cry for him for the rest of my life. I love Jason as a brother – but hate him for what he did. It's hard for me to understand how someone who was a very caring person as a boy could have grown up to do this." Mitchell's mother, Brenda Brooks, said in a statement: "We are all sad victims of this case. If Jason had been kept on the correct treatment this incident would never have happened. It must never be allowed to happen again." It was announced that Suffolk health authority was to hold an independent inquiry into the scandal, to be chaired by Louis Blom-Cooper, QC, and this was expected to last a fortnight.

Attacked Jim Powell told the *Mirror* how he had nearly become Mitchell's first murder victim. He was working at St Barnabas' church in Epsom, Surrey, when he was ambushed. "I thought I was a goner," he said. "He tried to hit me with a baseball bat, then came at me with two knives." Mitchell told police that his intended target had been the Rev. Michael Preston, but he couldn't find him and attacked Jim instead. "I've never seen anyone like him. I was lucky to escape with my life," said Jim. Mr Preston said he assumed Mitchell was homeless or a psychiatric patient when he let him shelter in the church from the rain. Mitchell then hid there overnight and attacked Mr Powell the following morning. "He could have killed Jim – but he ran for his life," Preston said.

Dr Ray Goddard, who had confirmed that Mitchell was fit to live in the community, also said he "posed no threat to himself or others". He continued: "His abnormal behaviour was the result of drug abuse, alcohol and a chaotic lifestyle. He has no underlying psychotic illness." Mitchell had been given anti-psychotic drugs which improved his "extremely disturbed" behaviour when he was sent to hospital in 1990. Dr Hadrian Bell diagnosed Mitchell after his arrest as "extremely dangerous", and Dr Goddard said: "I don't think it's appropriate to comment." He went on to say he would be happy to co-operate with the inquiry. Health boss David Long said:

"Everything about Mitchell's treatment seems to have been done properly – yet it all went terribly wrong. He was showing no signs of mental illness when discharge was considered. We have every confidence in Dr Goddard and his team." MIND director Ian Hartley said: "As far as we were concerned, Mitchell was a fairly ordinary young man."

The 1995 public inquiry heard how a "legal blunder" had led to Mitchell being freed. Counsel to the inquiry Oliver Thorold revealed that the discharge followed two "legally flawed" mental health review tribunals. The first said Mitchell's medication could be stopped. The Home Office ordered a second tribunal, after his behaviour deteriorated, but there was confusion as to what decisions had been made, and Mitchell was freed after "a sequence of misapprehensions", said Mr Thorold.

Dorangel Vargas
(1995)

Born into a poor family in Venezuela, Dorangel Vargas found himself living on the streets at an early age after his mother accused him of sexually abusing his younger sister. After being duped and raped by a man who had promised to help him, Vargas found himself living rough with few resources. He began a career of petty crime before turning to murder. In the city of San Cristobal, he began murdering and cannibalizing men – a deadly killing spree that lasted between

1995 and 1999. Dubbed the "Hannibal Lector of the Andes", he confessed at his arrest in February 1999 to eating up to 10 men during his four years of killing. He gave graphic accounts of the processes he went through to "prepare" the flesh of his victims, and stated: "Human meat is nice, but I also eat dogs, cats and lizards." He was also suspected of having cannibalized women, but there are those who did not believe his stories. Vargas was incarcerated for a short time, but one night suddenly disappeared from his cell. Many believed he had been set free, and rumours circulated that he had been made a scapegoat for a human trafficking ring.

Jarno Elg
(1998)

Jarno Elg was reported to have had a cruel and sadistic nature when it came to animals as a small child, regularly meting out horrendous violence to defenceless creatures. On one occasion he killed a dog by duct-taping it so it could not move and hitting it on a metal pipe.

In 1998, a dismembered leg was found at a rubbish dump; it was discovered to belong to a 23-year-old. The perpetrator Elg was tracked by police, and it transpired that on 21st November 1998, the Finnish youth had entered the house of his victim. The man was tortured and his head wrapped in duct tape in a satanic ritual. Two accomplices helped Elg to take various body parts from the man – who remained unnamed – which they ate before the victim was finally killed by strangulation.

Elg was eventually convicted of the young victim's murder alongside Terhi Johanna Tervashonka (17) and Mika Kristian Riska (21). The details of the case were sealed for at least four decades.

David Harker
(1999)

Cannibal killer David Harker chopped up his victim and ate part of her body with pasta and cheese, a court heard on 10th February 1999. And when doctors asked him about Hannibal Lecter in the film *The Silence of the Lambs*, he said chillingly: "People like me don't come from films – them films comes from people like me." Harker (24), who had the words "Subhuman" and "Disorder" tattooed on his scalp, claimed he strangled mother-of-four Julie Paterson with her tights after he "got bored" during a sex session. He told psychiatrists he then had sex with her body before chopping off her head and limbs, slicing flesh from her thigh, skinning it and cooking it with pasta and cheese sauce.

Harker dumped the 32-year-old's torso in a bin liner less than a mile from his bedsit; her head and limbs were left for collection by bin men. Later he bragged to friends about his horrific deed, but it was only when Julie's body was found weeks after she was reported missing and her picture was printed in a local paper that they alerted police to his claims. At first Harker denied the killing – only admitting it later when interviewed by three psychiatrists. A search of his flat in Darlington, County Durham found traces of Julie's blood and her tights. The 6ft 5in "monster" also bragged he was a serial killer. After Julie's death he boasted that he had killed two other people, one of whom was a homeless man in the North East.

Prosecutor Paul Worsley, QC, said police had investigated Harker's claims but could find no evidence. Mr Worsley said jobless Harker had fantasized about becoming a "notorious serial killer" for years. Witnesses told detectives he "avidly viewed" films about serial killers and read books on them. He boasted to friends that he "wanted to kill someone" and had erotic fantasies about mutilating bodies. Mr Worsley told Teesside Crown Court that Harker was "an extremely dangerous and evil man". The psychiatrists concluded he was "an extremely dangerous individual who had shown no remorse". Tests showed he was in the top four per cent of the most disturbed psychopaths. Aidan Marron, QC, defending, admitted: "He is a grossly disturbed individual. He is an intense and very dangerous psychopath. It seems inevitable that a life sentence must be imposed in a case such as this. He has experienced anxiety and has such a determination to change – it is now down to whether he has the ability to do that. He acknowledges the circumstances of his killing were both wicked and evil."

Harker denied murder, but admitted manslaughter on the grounds of diminished responsibility. He was jailed for life, with a recommendation that he served at least 14 years before being considered for parole. Mr Justice Bennett told him: "You have shown no remorse and I am satisfied you would kill again, given the slightest opportunity. You are an evil and extremely dangerous person." Harker, flanked by three officers in the dock, muttered "Thank you" when he heard the sentence.

Nathaniel Bar-Jonah
(2001)

A man was charged with murdering and eating a 10-year-old boy named Zachary Ramsey on 5th January 2001, amid fears that he was a serial killer who had preyed on dozens of children. The FBI confirmed that it had found a list of 54 other children, aged between five and 17, hidden inside Nathaniel Bar-Jonah's home in Montana. Agents tried to trace the people named on the list, dating back to the 1970s, to see if they were still alive. The case had a frightening similarity to that of Jeffrey Dahmer. Cops who raided the accused's home also found gruesome coded menus referring to cannibalizing children. Among the meals listed were 'barbecued kid', 'sex a la carte', 'my little kid dessert', 'little boy stew', 'little boy pot pies', and 'lunch is served on the patio with roasted child'. In other papers found by police, Bar-Jonah talked graphically about depraved sex acts. Police believed he was referring to actual events, in which Bar-Jonah molested Zachary, killed him, then served his remains to friends in burgers and stews. Investigators removed tens of thousands of photos of local children clipped from newspapers.

They also found two yearbooks from a local primary school, stun guns, knives, batons, police badges and a toy chrome pistol.

Bar-Jonah moved to the mountains of Montana in 1991 when he was freed from jail after kidnapping two boys in his home state of Massachusetts. FBI agents discovered that he had an obsession with sexual violence and cannibalism. Zachary had vanished on his way to school four years before his murderer's arrest, and his body had never been found. Friends of Bar-Jonah told investigators that the suspect served them meals in which the meat tasted strange. His brother, who refused to give his name, said: "A lot of people think the family knew about Nathan, but there's a whole bunch we don't know. We pray it's not true, but they have a lot of evidence. We don't condone anything Nathan may have done and we haven't interfered with police." His sister added: "We feel awful. Nate's very sick and he needs help."

Bar-Jonah was convicted of kidnapping, aggravated assault and sexual assault, and given a 130-year prison sentence. He maintained his innocence until his death in 2008.

Katherine Knight
(2001)

Jilted Katherine Knight stabbed her lover, cut off his skin, then cooked his chopped-up body and served it on dinner plates. Knight – a boner and slicer at an abattoir – left the skin hanging in the hall and the plates in the kitchen, with the names of John Price's three children next to them.

Earlier, mother of four Knight (44) made a home video for her teenage children, outlining her plans to slaughter Mr Price, her lover of six years. Then she went to his home, where she found him unconscious – believed to be because of a drug overdose – and killed him. Using her abattoir skills and tools, she cut off his head and boiled it with body parts and vegetables. The scenes in the house were so gruesome that police officers were still receiving counselling a year later, a court heard in East Maitland, near Sydney on 19th October 2001. Knight admitted murder, sparing Mr Price's children, John (28), Rosemary (27), and Rebecca (16), from hearing further horrific details. Rosemary said later: "It would have haunted the jury for the rest of their lives like it haunts us.

"Only a week before Dad's death they were at a family celebration for a grandchild's birthday. Everything seemed OK between them. We had no idea what was to come. Apparently Dad wanted out of the relationship. He had applied for an aggravated violence order against her because he was frightened of what she might do. For her to do what she did to him makes it really hard to bear.

"Dad was a great bloke, a grandfather who loved a laugh and a good time. He didn't deserve this."

Knight was sentenced to life in prison, and because of the severity of her crimes and lack of remorse her papers were marked "never to be released". She was the first Australian woman to be sentenced to life imprisonment without parole.

Armin Meiwes

(2001)

Many people find it hard to believe that anyone would respond to an advertisement asking for a willing victim to be slaughtered. But that is exactly what happened in the case of Armin Meiwes in 2001. German-born Meiwes advertised on an internet site looking for a well-built man, aged between 18 and 30, who was willing to be killed and consumed, after another German had said he couldn't go through with the plan. He posted: "I need a REAL victim".

He received a response from a man who was prepared to die for him, and the two men met on Christmas Day 2001, Brandes saying: "I am your flesh." A horrendous videotape of unimaginable acts, including cannibalism, was eventually found after Meiwes revealed details of his crime.

The dead man was named as Bernd Juergen Brandes (42). The State Prosecutor in Kassel, Germany, said little evidence was left because Meiwes had eaten most of the body. It was revealed that the killer had frozen Brandes' body parts into bite-sized pieces that he could snack on. The 41-year-old IT specialist had made burgers out of the man's shoulder flesh, steaks from his buttocks and stews from his stomach and thighs, police said. He admitted that the pair had dined on Bernd's severed penis, after which Meiwes had stabbed his victim and dismembered him, videotaping the murder. Bisexual Bernd had been more than willing to be the victim, and the accused claimed that he had been obsessed with the idea of being eaten alive since watching *The Silence of the Lambs*. Meiwes told the magazine *Stern* that he plied Brandes with brandy and tranquillizers before cutting off his penis and frying it in a pan with garlic, salt and pepper. He said they both ate the organ, which had "shrivelled up and wasn't very tasty". Afterwards he felt "fulfilled, like I was married or something". It took Bernd almost 10 hours to die – from the time his penis was severed to the time his killer repeatedly plunged the blade into the victim's throat. Meiwes had then stuffed 65lbs of flesh – which he labelled rump, steak, fillet, ham and bacon – into his freezer. He later cooked some body parts on his garden barbecue. Meiwes told police: "The flesh tasted so much like pork, I can't tell you."

Meiwes was arrested after he posted an internet advert looking for a second man, and was charged with murder. Police tracked him down after a student alerted them to the advert.

Prosecutor Hans-Manfred Jung said: "It is certain that the crime was committed with the agreement of the victim." But he added that Meiwes had been charged with murder because evidence showed he had taken the first step.

After Bernd's death, a London man had answered Meiwes' second internet request and visited his home. He was wrapped in cellophane and his body parts were marked out for butchering, but he pulled out of the "sick stunt" at the last minute and Meiwes let him go. He then rejected another Londoner because his body was "too fatty".

Shocking details of Meiwes' flesh-eating were revealed in July 2003 before his murder trial, which was planned for August. He told police he had dreamt of eating a human since he was 12, and had imagined putting a friend on a spit to "slowly roast". He had prepared a room at his shambolic farmhouse as a butchery – it had a wooden cage to secure his victims. Police found recipes at his home for human flesh, including penis in red wine and breaded young man's liver.

When Meiwes went on trial on 3rd December 2003, it was Europe's first case involving cannibalism. Brandes' former girlfriend, Bettina (30), was expected to give evidence. She said that the couple had enjoyed a normal relationship until he had answered Meiwes' advertisement. Meiwes denied murder, because he said that Bernd died of his own free will. He told the court that killing Bernd was the fulfillment of a "lifelong dream" for both of them. "I couldn't regret it because this is what we both wanted. That is why I am not guilty of murder – I helped a man fulfill his biggest wish too." He said that he had rejected one man because "he wanted me to burn his balls with a flamethrower and hammer his body down with nails and pins while he was whipped to death … I found that a bit weird." The judges were shown the video, which was Exhibit A, but it was deemed so grisly that the press and public were excluded. Scenes showed Bernd undressing, then instructing Meiwes to cut off his penis – which he did with an 18-inch butcher's knife. After eating it, Bernd was left to bleed for hours while his abuser watched a Disney film. Meiwes then returned and stabbed his victim in the throat.

At Christmas 2003, Meiwes sickened prison staff when he demanded an eight-inch Bockwurst sausage be cooked in garlic and white wine. An official said he could have the sausage, but that it wouldn't be prepared that way. Back in court in January 2004, it was revealed that the killer had turned his home into a shrine after the death of his mother, Waldtrud. He dressed up in her clothes and imitated her voice – just like Norman Bates in the Hitchcock film *Psycho*. One of his former schoolfriends said that the killer had been dominated by his mother all his life. "Her word was law. She towered over him in death as well as in life," said Berthold Sieberg. The court also heard how Meiwes' depravity had its roots in horrific make-believe games that he played as a child. Even at an age of supposed innocence, he had harboured a desire to take life. He tore Barbie dolls apart, to mimic dismemberment, at the age of 10. At 11, while other boys collected bubble gum cards and football magazines, he smeared himself in tomato ketchup and imagined that he had been freshly butchered. He invented an imaginary friend – Franky – a name he later used to seek out his victim. Of his mother's death, Meiwes said: "I was all alone in the world ... and the fantasies became stronger and stronger and the need to satisfy them also became stronger." He began collecting ever more violent pornographic pictures and gruesome images from the internet, including torture scenes that he would watch for hours, while committing a lone sex act.

Psychologists told the eight-week trial more about Meiwes' tortured relationship with his domineering mother, which had developed after his father left home when the boy was nine. The self-confessed bisexual, spoken of by women as gentle, went out on ordinary dates, but came home to baked marzipan dolls – shaped as anatomically correct males – which he ritually "killed" before eating.

The panel of three judges caused astonishment when they returned a verdict of guilty of manslaughter. The accused remained impassive as the verdict was passed. President of the court Judge Volker Muetze said the fact that both men were "severely psychologically disturbed" made it a complex case. "He didn't kill out of sexual gratification, but because he wanted to slaughter and eat a man." Doctors had decided that Meiwes was sane at the time of the killing. Legal experts had expected nothing less than murder, as far as the verdict was concerned; they were not convinced Bernd truly wanted to die. Cannibalism expert Jacques Buval said: "Cannibalism is like paedophilia. It is in him. You can't cure it. He will want to do it again."

Meiwes was retried in 2006 and received a life sentence. The appeal by prosecutors said the original eight-year sentence for manslaughter was totally unsatisfactory. The trial highlighted the sick chatrooms where cannibals and victims "meet". Police hoped the tougher sentence would send a message to all potential cannibals that consent from a victim was not a licence to kill.

Bernd was described as having died in great pain.

Yoo Young-chul

(2003)

By 2003, police in South Korea knew they were dealing with a cannibal serial killer. Between that year and the next, 21 people were murdered. The victims – many of whom were prostitutes or wealthy old men – had been slain with a hammer, decapitated, mutilated and eaten.

The suspect and eventually convicted killer was Yoo Young-chul, a man who had grown up in poverty with his father. After his arrest, it was revealed that the cannibal had eaten the flesh and raw livers of many of his victims. He was sentenced to death in 2005, which led to capital punishment being retained in South Korea. Just before this, the country had been debating whether to abolish the death sentence, but the Young-chul murders fuelled the argument in favour of maintaining it, so heinous were his crimes.

Victim's Mother Sues Cannibal

(2003)

Rap star Antron "Big Lurch" Singleton ate the lungs of a woman he allegedly stabbed to death, according to a lawsuit filed by the victim's mother, Carolyn Stinson. He was said to have been high on the drug PCP when he attacked roommate Tynisha Ysais in Los Angeles. Her lungs were found in Singleton's stomach. Stinson claimed that Death Row Records gave him PCP to make him a better gangsta rapper.

Congo Troops Eat Pygmies
(2003)

UN officials said they had evidence that Congolese soldiers had killed and eaten Pygmies in January 2003. Rebel groups often hired the forest tribesmen to hunt for their food while they concentrated on fighting, but, said the officials, if the bushmen returned empty-handed they were killed and eaten. Manodje Mounoubai of the UN mission said: "We've sent a team of six to investigate these reports of cannibalism." An official of the Congolese Rally for Democracy-Liberation said that refugees had also reported that Pygmies were being forced to feed on their fellow tribesmen.

In May 2003 it was announced that Tony Blair was considering a United Nations request to boost peacekeepers in one of Africa's bloodiest civil wars, in the Congo – where up to three million had died since 1988. The British Prime Minister told the Commons: "We are seeing, given all our other engagements, what support we can give." The majority of the force was expected to be made up of French soldiers, but Ministry of Defence sources said they expected the British contribution to be "substantial". The troops were to be based in the town of Bunia after fighting had left at least 280 dead. It was reported that fighters had patrolled the streets with human organs hanging from their weapons. The Hema and Lendu tribes were battling for control of vast mineral deposits and forests. A spokesman said the killings had to stop.

Three months later, a reporter in the *Mirror* said: "The 15-year-old boy bites into a packet of jelly babies as he tells me how he killed. First there were the mothers, after he'd raped them. Then their babies. Four of them. The eldest aged three. He speaks softly, with great precision, about what he did. Then he wanders off, having thanked me for the sweets, to play marbles with the other killers.

"He is the oldest of 39 boys in this dusty compound. Laughing, boisterous kids who have seen and exacted horror beyond imagining. They assemble for a school photo, jostling for position. A barked order and they suddenly freeze. Attention. Awaiting command, soldiers again."

Frozen on film was the class of child soldiers who, according to their teachers, had murdered at least 106 people. The boys, many recruited at the age of 10 and younger, were being demobbed as part of a Save the Children initiative set up in the lakeside town of Bukavu in South Kivu, part of the Great Lakes region of central Africa. This was the area, in the eastern Democratic Republic of the Congo, which had seen continuous fighting for the previous five years. It was where four million people had died – the greatest human toll since the Second World War – and 10 million people had been forced to flee their homes.

In July 2003, 70 British Army engineers arrived in the country (about the size of Western Europe) as part of the international peace effort. Their duty was painfully brief. There were none of the self-interested reasons that had fired the invasions of Iraq and Afghanistan, or the wars against Milosevic and Saddam. There were no terrorists plotting outrage in London or New York and no weapons of mass destruction, real or imagined. Uganda and Rwanda, the neighbouring countries which had sparked the conflict over one of the world's richest territories, had withdrawn – leaving local militia to fight a proxy war for them. Children with Kalashnikovs ran amok.

It was the armed kids that formed the front line – they were the weapons of mass destruction. Anisette Birindwa, whom the journalist spoke to, was one among thousands. In Africa, children were killing children in huge numbers, and had done for years. Many were orphans, homeless and hungry. And so they became soldiers, because soldiers had guns, and guns guaranteed food and shelter. In return, they were sent forward first into appallingly fierce and bloody battles, because children did not understand the consequences of their actions. They had been brainwashed.

The journalist wrote: "Modern weapons, light, easy to use are child's play. Bang, bang – you're dead. Two kids standing little more than an arm's length from each other, blowing themselves to pieces. And so Anisette tells me his story. He was 12 when the soldiers came. His home outside Bukavu was destroyed by troops from Rwanda, or maybe it was the Interahamwe – the escaping army which was responsible for the murder of 800,000 Tutsis before the new, post-genocidal Rwanda was formed nine years ago. Or maybe it was 'just Tutsis'. Anisette isn't sure because they're all the same to him. Starving, parentless, he joined the M-40 militia which, he believed, was fighting for his homeland. He says he trained as a nurse. But no ordinary nurse. He was taught magic remedies. His medicine could turn bullets into water and make his mates invincible. He was a big shot.

"He tells me: 'One day, we captured two women, the wives of the Interahamwe, and the commander told me to kill them. Six of us raped them. Then we stabbed them to death with machetes. It was cheaper than bullets. They begged us to spare them, but we laughed. We had orders. We cut out their hearts to take to the commander. Their babies were aged three months, a boy; a one-year-old girl; another boy, two; and the last aged three. We killed them and used their bodies to make medicine. I boiled their feet and arms to grind and put in bottles. The potion has the power to stop bullets. I burned the meat into ash which you sprinkle on your body to give extra strength. The heads of the children and their mothers we gave to the commander. We ate the hearts, kidneys and livers.' He named the commander as Kahasha, whose nickname was Fokamike."

The journalist said that perhaps one day the man would be tried for war crimes. Anisette had been delivered to the demob centre after being arrested by Rwandan-backed RCD soldiers. The social workers offered his community a grant to help rebuild their village in the hope that it would stop them from returning to war. Boys were walking around with scars on their chests, gouged to ward off bullets. The journalist heard one child, aged 12, say he was happy that he fired his gun and "the big enemy man flopped". Girls fared no better. Feza Mateso (13) had been taken by the M-40 soldiers two years before. She said: "Mummy pleaded, offering five goats instead. They took the goats as well. They made me the wife of a commander called Justin. He wanted sex too much. I was afraid, but after seven months I ran away, stealing a canoe to cross the river south of Bukavu. Another commander called Shakale found me and he started to use me. Then the RCD attacked and I was arrested, taken to Kavumu, north of the city, and raped and raped. There were five girls there. Three men took each of us. They used me up to seven times a day for two weeks. When I became sick they left me outside the hospital."

The young girl began to cough as she walked with the journalist to the lake. Beside its tranquil beauty she began to look like a child again. In Africa they didn't like to talk about HIV and Aids, but the "girl soldiers" weren't tested. Feza stumbled around as she coughed and coughed and coughed: it seemed that the inevitable had happened.

In Goma, the journalist met a friend of Feza's, Mashuruliko Mgoyi (13), who joined the militia when she was just 10. She was captured by the RCD and used by commander, Gere Kola, as a wife. "When he didn't use me, he put me in the front line. The first man I killed was militia. I was told to fire two bullets in the air and then two at his feet. Then I shot him in the chest. I had to do this because they said he had special powers and a single shot would not kill him. Then

I had to cut off his head, make a fire and burn the body and head separately. I was glad they blindfolded the man before I killed him. He was crying, offering to tell us where his comrades were hiding, but they said kill him anyway, so I did.

"One day I was sent to fetch water. A soldier came the other way and ordered me into the long grass, where he raped me. When he finished, five of his friends had me. I was left lying there in terrible pain. I could feel the hurt in my womb. It was like wounds." Doctors found that she was suffering from a variety of sexually transmitted diseases. She also had TB, and maybe HIV or Aids, but they wouldn't test for that. Despite all this, "Marshy" was happy. She had just been reunited with her father, whom she hadn't seen since she was five years old: Save the Children had traced him and four of her brothers and sisters. He told her to stop being a soldier and to go and live with him. "I will never go back to the army," she said. "I want to get rid of those dreams. I close my eyes and see bad spirits, the face of that blindfolded man, the people I killed in battle, many of them."

The journalist travelled on dirt roads to the Bunia front line, which Uganda and Rwanda had helped to create. French soldiers had, by this time, secured the town. "Sembo Mateso is 17, the obvious top cat among the 11 boys being demobbed by SC-UK. 'Yes, I killed,' he said. 'I cut off limbs and ate body parts. We were hungry and we had orders.' He and his friend were arrested and handed over by the French, who found them carrying a hand grenade and a mobile phone ... There are 20,000 refugees in the two camps ... There are children whose arms have been cut off. Women with internal injuries

... And next door there are the young orphans covered in scabies, such as three-year-old Patience, who was found, half-dead, under her mother's corpse."

The country was filled with "children with guns, scavenging and killing and maiming and cannibalizing to order. One at least, wears the testicles of a UN soldier they captured, brandishing them as a talisman. Another remembers the taste of his liver. A third has tied another UN soldier's penis to his wrist. Others simply stubbed their ganja butts on the mutilated bodies."

While Iraq and Afghanistan had hit the headlines in Europe over the previous two years, the dying in the Congo went unheard.

A Fijian Apology
(2003)

The *Mirror* reported in October 2003 that a tribe in Fiji was to apologize 136 years after eating a Methodist missionary who insulted a chief by touching his head. The people of Navosa, on the island Viti Levu, wanted to say sorry to his descendants, hoping it would lift the "curse" on their district. Minister Thomas Baker was served up to villagers with a sweet tomato relish following his fatal error in 1867. His family were asked to attend a ceremony in the mountain settlement, hosted by the tribal chief Ratu Filimoni. Fiji's prime minister, Laisenia Qarase, was also expected to attend. The missionary met his end when he sailed to the tiny Pacific island to try to convert the natives to Christianity. At first he was well received by the Navatusila tribe in their remote district, but in his ignorance of local custom, he touched the chief's head when trying to retrieve a comb he had left in his hut. He was doomed.

According to folklore, Chief Navatusila told him: "The sun will rise tomorrow. You won't see it." The vicar was stripped naked, decapitated and ritually boiled. His clothes were also cooked. "We ate every part of him except his boots," one villager recorded for the history books. His surviving footwear was much later housed in a museum in Fiji's capital Suva, along with the pot he was cooked in and the axe that killed him. The incident was so well known that author Jack London wrote a short story about it, *The Whale Tooth*.

Although it is still frowned upon to touch heads, there was little danger of Mr Baker's descendants meeting the same fate – the former British colony had given up cannibalism more than 100 years before when its people converted to Christianity and Hinduism. An official said: "Tourists shouldn't be put off. There hasn't been a cannibal here since the 19th century. These days we prefer chicken."

Paul Durant
(2004)

A fugitive held over the murder of his British girlfriend in Spain confessed to eating her body. Armed robber Paul Durant told how he had cut up Karen Durrell and devoured some of her remains before disposing of what was left in bin bags around the town where she lived. In a letter to the *Mirror* written in his prison cell on the Costa Blanca, the 44-year-old admitted he cut his girlfriend into small parts and ate her after killing her at her flat in Calpe, 15 miles from Benidorm, having been driven to do so by messages from God arriving via his television. Heroin addict Durant added: "I ate what part of her I found eatable."

Durant told how he believed his victim had been delivered to him by God to be chopped up and eaten. The deranged man killed Karen within days of their meeting. He was arrested in March 2004 over the divorced mum's murder, but his sensational confession that he ate the 41-year-old shocked and sickened locals – and confirmed detectives' worst fears. "I finally disposed of what was left in small rubbish bags around Calpe," the letter continued. "Before I killed Karen I told her I had come to Spain where I was going to kill and eat paedophiles. My mental state was breaking down at this stage. I believe she knew she had to die. I know I badly need help. I find it very hard to speak about my crime. I was only violent to her once and that was when I killed her."

Durant even claimed he had told police in Britain of his cannibal tendencies after several arrests during a criminal career that stretched over three decades. He said: "I had a previous desire to kill and eat people and told the British police so when I was held in the past." Spanish police were alerted when Karen's family could not get hold of her. When officers burst into her third-storey apartment they discovered that she had been stabbed to death and her body cut up.

They found pools of blood in a bath, blood-stained knives and a saw with human tissue on its blade. A suitcase belonging to her that was heavily stained with blood was discovered in a bedroom. Detectives spent weeks searching dustbins and rubbish heaps in the area but found no trace of Karen's body or of her pet terrier Louis. Durant made no mention of the dog in his confession, but police believed that he suffered the same fate as his owner.

When Durant was arrested he told officers: "I have committed many more crimes." He was already suspected of other killings by Scotland Yard when he fled to Spain in December 2003. Durant had been held just before Christmas in a Flying Squad ambush as he tried to snatch bags containing £38,000 from a guard outside a post office in Whitechapel, East London. There was a violent struggle, during which a replica pistol was wrestled from his grasp. He claimed he had been injured as police overpowered him, and he was taken to the nearby Royal London Hospital for X-rays. Two policemen stood guard outside his ward, but he gave them the slip by climbing 40 feet down the side of the hospital when he went for a cigarette. He said: "I scaled the balcony. I escaped out of fear of going back to prison again. I have been in and out of institutions since the age of 11." During the 1980s and 1990s Durant had carried out a string of armed robberies on Post Office vans and security trucks, netting around £500,000, and had served two jail terms. He was also thought to have been involved in the drug trade, and was the main suspect in the murder of a drug dealer at Stepney in the 1990s.

Durant, from East London, left Britain using a false passport and made his way overland to Spain in stolen cars and on buses and trains. By February he had arrived in Calpe, where he befriended Karen and her lover Miles Lanning. The trio started drinking together before Durant muscled in on Karen. Miles (37) said he had warned Karen, of Barking in East London, that there was something odd about their new friend. He said the fugitive stole his girlfriend, then threatened to kill him if he interfered. Miles added: "I told her Durant was a weirdo loner and I warned her to steer clear of him, but she seemed to feel sorry for him. He was grooming her. It was obvious he had his sights on her. He drove a wedge between us. We were short of money. I flew home to England to raise some more cash and as soon as I had gone he moved into our apartment. One evening there was a message on my answering machine from Durant.

"He said he thought I was a prick for going back to England and if I came back he would kill me. But within a week he had killed her ... He would just laugh to himself about nothing into thin air. It was a mad laugh ... I carried her suitcase from the airport. The idea that he chopped her up and put her in that suitcase, it's all I can think about."

Durant's confession of cannibalism sparked a new murder probe in Britain in 2004. Scotland Yard was to investigate links to the killing of the drug dealer in Stepney, while the Guardia Civil studied details of a letter sent by the crazed killer as to the whereabouts of his victim's remains. A Scotland Yard source said: "We are examining links to other crimes ... in light of subsequent events." A Spanish police source said: "He has fallen into silence, and so anything like

A cannibal head-hunter of the Dani tribe in Dutch New Guinea, July 1962.

Robert Maudsley was jailed for life in 1974 after he garrotted a labourer, but three years later he was transferred to Broadmoor where he killed a paedophile. According to a guard, Maudsley cracked the man's skull open "like a boiled egg" and ate part of his brain with a spoon.

President of Uganda General Idi Amin waves goodbye as he boards his plane to return to Uganda following his visit to Zaire in July 1975. Within two years President Amin was accused of cannibalism, when his former personal doctor said the Ugandan dictator ate part of the liver from one of his dead ministers.

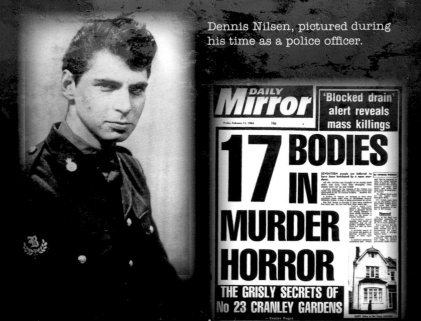

Dennis Nilsen, pictured during his time as a police officer.

The Mirror front page on 11th February 1983 broke the news of Dennis Nilsen's horrific killing spree.

Plastic covers in the garden of 195 Melrose Avenue in February 1983. This is where mass murderer Dennis Nilsen killed some of his many victims.

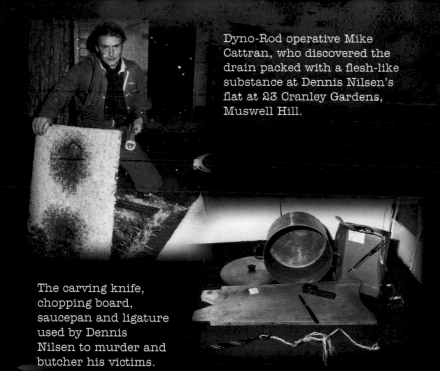

Dyno-Rod operative Mike Cattran, who discovered the drain packed with a flesh-like substance at Dennis Nilsen's flat at 23 Cranley Gardens, Muswell Hill.

The carving knife, chopping board, saucepan and ligature used by Dennis Nilsen to murder and butcher his victims.

Dennis Nilsen – under arrest – is led from a prison van by police in February 1983.

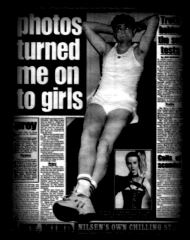

photos turned me on to girls

NILSEN'S OWN CHILLING ST

Dennis Nilsen pictured in April 1995 at Whitemoor jail, where he was shown erotic images as part of tests into his mental state.

THE CANNIBAL

Face of madman who killed 17 and ate them

THIS is the face of real-life Silence Of The Lambs killer Jeffrey Dahmer who has confessed to butchering 17 men.

Police believe the blood-mad man many of his victims while they were still alive - just like Hannibal the Cannibal in the hit movie.

Yesterday, the 31-year-old factory worker appeared in a Wisconsin court accused of four murders - with more death charges expected to follow.

As the unshaven killer was making his brief appearance before the US judge, yet more grisly details of his horrific life were revealed by his step-mother Shari.

She told how her husband once found bones in a massive vat at a flat where their son often slept.

Smell

"We smelled a harsh odour coming from the basement flat," she said.

"His father Lionel investigated and found bones and residue in a huge vat.

"He couldn't tell if they were human or animal.

From STEWART DICKSON in New York

Jeffrey said it was an animal he had found.

"Ever since he was young he liked to see and to scrape the meat off dead animals."

And Shari told how to the flat in his grandmother's house.

Torture

"One time he was there with a man when his grandmother opened the door.

"She could see only in her bare chest. He warned her: 'You don't want them to come down here'

"She thought they were naked so she didn't go down.

Police found several heads, torsos, boxes of body parts and photos and videos of tortured victims in Dahmer's apartment.

The sick killer was arrested after an intended victim escaped and was found by police running down the street - his hands still handcuffed.

'Butcher' link on air base

CANNIBAL Jeffrey Dahmer is suspected of killing five women in Germany while serving with US forces.

The women were all murdered and their bodies mutilated near an air base where he was stationed as a medical orderly more than ten years ago.

A public prosecutor in the town of Bad Kreuznach told a German newspaper yesterday: "We have a burning interest in this Dahmer. We are checking to see if he could be the killer."

He said there were similarities between the murders even though all the German victims were women and only men were murdered in Milwaukee.

Dubbed the "real-life *Silence of the Lambs* killer", Jeffrey Dahmer confessed in 1991 to butchering 17 men.

Already serving life, Christopher Scarver told a court in December 1994 how he smashed serial killer Jeffrey Dahmer over the head with a steel bar then left him gurgling on the floor because God had told him to do it.

Cannibal's killer

By MARK DOWDNEY
Foreign Editor

SHACKLED lifer Christopher Scarver is led away by police after telling how he bludgeoned to death cannibal killer Jeffrey Dahmer in jail.

Scarver, 25, smashed the mass killer over the head with a steel bar and told detectives: "I left him gurgling on the floor because

God told me to do it." Scarver, who once claimed to be the son of God, briefly appeared in court yesterday, accused of murdering Dahmer, 34, and another prisoner Jesse An-

derson at Portage jail in Wisconsin two weeks ago.

Dahmer, who killed 17 young men and boys in an orgy of gay sex and cannibalism, was murdered with a 20inch bar stolen from the prison gym.

A judge ordered mental tests on Scarver.

SHOOT THE RED RIPPER!

SINISTER: Monster Chikatilo is found guilty

Evil grandfather Andrei Chikatilo was known as the Rostov Ripper after slaughtering 21 boys, 14 girls and 17 women in Russia during the 1980s and 1990s. In 1992, he was found guilty of 52 murders.

A REAL-LIFE Hannibal "The Cannibal" Lecter gave a sinister smile yesterday as he was found guilty of 52 murders.

By MARK DOWDNEY
Foreign Editor

Gouged

Dear deer

LAMBS KILLER

MEDICAL REPORT BY DR RAYMOND GODDARD

He's a pleasant young man with no sign of malice

DECISION: Dr Ray Goddard

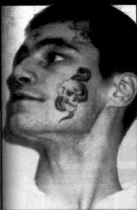

CAGED AT LAST: Tattooed monster Jason Mitchell got three life sentences for his horrific crimes

Beating

Voices

Sound

Ordinary

I was nearly first victim

Jason Mitchell received three life sentences for his crimes in 1995. The tattooed monster had planned to kill and eat a pensioner couple but decided against it because they were too old.

CANNIBAL KILLER
Psychopath chopped up body and cooked it with pasta

By PATRICK MULCHRONE

CANNIBAL killer David Harker chopped up his victim and ate part of her body with pasta and cheese, a court heard yesterday.

And when doctors asked him about Hannibal Lecter in the film Silence of the Lambs, he said chillingly: "People like me don't come from films — films come from people like me."

Madman Harker, 24, who has the words "Subhuman" and "Disorder" tattooed on his scalp, claimed he strangled mother-of-four Julie Paterson with her tights after he "got bored" during a sex romp.

He told psychiatrists he then had sex with her body before chopping off her head and limbs, slicing flesh from her thigh, skinning it and cooking it with pasta and cheese sauce.

Blood

He dumped 32-year-old Julie's torso in a binliner less than a mile from his bedsit. Her head and limbs were left for collection by dustmen.

Later he bragged to friends about his horrific deed.

But it was only when Julie's body was found weeks after she was reported missing and her picture was printed in a local paper that they alerted police to his claims.

At first Harker denied the killing — only admitting it later when interviewed by three psychiatrists.

A search of his flat in Darlington, Co Durham, found traces of Julie's blood and her tights. The 6ft 1in monster also bragged he was a serial killer, it was said.

After Julie's death he boasted that he had killed two other people, one a tramp-like man in the North East.

Prosecutor Paul Worsley QC told police he had investigated his claims but could find no evidence.

Mr Worsley said jobless Harker had fantasised about becoming a "notorious serial killer" for years. Witnesses told detectives he "avidly viewed" films about serial killers and read books on them.

He boasted to friends that he "wanted to kill someone" and had erotic fantasies about mutilating bodies.

Mr Worsley told Teesside Crown Court that Harker is "an extremely dangerous and evil man".

The psychiatrists concluded he was "an extremely dangerous individual who had shown no remorse".

He told them his favourite films were Henry: Portrait Of A Serial Killer and A Clockwork Orange.

Their tests showed he was in the top four per cent of the most disturbed psychopaths.

Aidan Marron QC, defending, admitted: "He is a grossly disturbed individual.

"He is an intense and very dangerous psychopath." H

sentence must be imposed in a case such as this.

"He has experienced anxiety and has such a determination to change — it is now down to whether he has the ability to do that.

"He acknowledges the circumstances of his killing were both wicked and evil."

Harker denied murder but admitted manslaughter on the grounds of diminished responsibility.

recommendation that he serves at least 14 years before being considered for parole.

Mr Justice Bennett told him: "You have shown no remorse and I am satisfied you would kill again, given the slightest opportunity.

"You are an evil and extremely dangerous person."

Harker, flanked by three officers in the dock, muttered "Thank you" when he h

VICTIM: Mum-of-four Julie Paterson was throttled with tights

EVIL: Madman David Harker boasted of being serial killer

David Harker chopped up his victim, mum-of-four Julie Paterson, and ate part of her flesh after cooking it with pasta and a cheese sauce.

When Nathan Bar-Jonah was arrested in January 2001 charged with murdering and eating a 10-year-old boy in the United States, the FBI feared that his killing spree could total more than 50 children.

NATHANIEL THE CANNIBAL
He may have eaten dozens of kids

EXCLUSIVE from ANDY LINES
US Editor in New York

A MANIAC charged with murdering and eating a 10-year-old boy was last night feared to be a serial killer who preyed on dozens of children.

Nathaniel Bar-Jonah is accused of torturing Zachary Ramsey before cooking his body and serving bits of it to meals to neighbours.

The FBI confirmed yesterday that it had found a list of other children, aged between five and 17, hidden inside his home in Montana.

Agents are trying to trace the people on the list, daring back to the Seventies, to see if they are alive.

The case has frightening similarities to that of notorious cannibal Jeffrey Dahmer, who killed 17 young men and ate them.

Cops who raided Bar-Jonah's home in Montana yesterday found what they believe to be a list of up to 22 children he is suspected of kidnapping.

Among the meals he listed were barbecued spare ribs, boiled chicken, roast and human stew. Little boy pot pies, and spicy lunch is served on the patio with roasted child.

In other papers found by police Bar-Jonah also talked graphically about depraved sex acts.

Police believe these refer to actual events where Bar-Jonah molested Ramsey, killed him, then served his remains to friends in burgers and stew.

Investigators recovered tens of thousands of photos of local children clipped from newspapers.

They also found two yearbooks from a local primary school, stun guns, knives, balloons, police badges and a toy gun.

Bar-Jonah moved to the mountains of Montana in 1991 when he was freed from jail after kidnapping two boys in his home state of Massachusetts.

Now FBI agents have discovered that he has an obsession with sexual violence and cannibalism.

Zachary vanished on his way to school four years ago and has never been found.

Friends of Bar-Jonah told investigators that the suspect served them meals at the most important.

His brother, who helped in his life name, said: "A lot of people think the family knew about what Nathan's doing, a whole bunch we don't know.

"We pray it's not true, but there's a lot of evidence. We don't condone anything Nathan may have done and we haven't interfered with police.

He once again: "we all came, knew a very sick soul and he never but h

VILLAIN: Bar-Jonah is said to have preyed on children

ORDEAL: Zachary

German-born Armin Meiwes advertised on an internet site looking for a well-built man aged between 18 and 30 willing to be killed and consumed. He found a willing participant.

When Meiwes went on trial on 3rd December 2003, it was Europe's first case involving cannibalism.

DAILY Mirror 3-PAGE SPECIAL REPORT

Child killers of the Congo

ANTON ANTONOWICZ on Africa's worst tragedy

Even children caught up in one of Africa's bloodiest civil wars in the Congo at the beginning of the 21st century were not immune from committing atrocities including cannibalism.

The front page of the *Mirror* of 20th February 2004 asks the disturbing question whether mental patient Peter Bryan was a cannibal.

DAILY Mirror

NEWSPAPER OF THE YEAR · 32p

Friday February 20 2004

SHOWBIZ EXCLUSIVE.. I WANT A £1M BRA FOR MY 18th

ANOTHER SHOWBIZ EXCLUSIVE..
I couldn't keep my hands off Justin's body..
WE TRACK DOWN TIMBERLAKE'S BRITS GIRL: PAGE 3

FACE OF A CANNIBAL?

Accused had just been let out of mental hospital

BLOODY BLUNDER

Covered in his victim's blood.. but Broadmoor nurse simply helped cannibal clean himself up

By GARY JONES

A STRING of errors that allowed cannibal killer Peter Bryan to roam free are to be investigated by three separate inquiries.

One will want to know why nurses at Broadmoor hospital cleaned up the blood-stained monster after he had attacked patient Richard Loudwell.

Bryan, pictured above, calmly told staff, who also put his bloody clothes in the laundry: "I have harmed myself."

A nurse revealed: "He was extremely persuasive."

Loudwell, 60, was found later, with a pyjama cord around his neck and serious head injuries. He died two months later.

Bryan, 35, was initially sent to

SCENE: Broadmoor where Bryan struck

pleased. He was then moved to an open psychiatric ward in East London.

During day leave he killed pal Brian Cherry, 43, who lived close by, sawed off his arms and left leg and fried and ate his brain.

Bryan was sent to Broadmoor hospital, with a recommendation he be locked up in the most secure part.

But he was put in medium security where he throttled killer Loudwell.

The first inquiry will examine the "care and treatment" of Loudwell until his admission to Broadmoor.

Another will concentrate on the treatment of Bryan and his contact with mental health experts before the killing of Mr Cherry.

The third will look at how Loudwell and Bryan came to be admitted to

Broadmoor and their treatment there. The first report is expected within six months. A Broadmoor spokeswoman said: "We'll be looking very closely at what went wrong and make recommendations.

"We cannot comment further until the inquiry reports are published.

The three-part investigation is one of the biggest-ever into mental health services and will cost tens of thousands of pounds.

An executive summary will be published once all three inquiries have reached their final conclusions.

● NEW legislation to give greater protection to the public rather than the rights of patients is to be considered by the Government.

A damning verdict on the decision to allow Peter Bryan day leave from a psychiatric ward in East London, which allowed him to kill, cook and eat a supposed friend.

A shocking confession in October 2004 as deranged killer Paul Durant admitted eating his girlfriend Karen Durrell.

DAILY Mirror

Thursday October 7 2004

www.mirror.co.uk 35p

RED IN LOVE

EXCLUSIVE: PAGE 11

How to beat breast cancer

bodytalk

SEE PAGE 33

BRUTAL KILLER'S SHOCKING CONFESSION TO THE MIRROR

I'VE EATEN MY GIRLFRIEND

EXCLUSIVE

By JEFF EDWARDS Chief Crime Correspondent

A FUGITIVE held over the murder of his British girlfriend in Spain has confessed to eating her body.

Armed robber Paul Durant told how he cut up Karen Durrell and devoured some of her remains before disposing of what was left in bin bags around the town where they lived.

In a letter to the Mirror from his prison cell on the Costa Blanca, the 51-year-old said he "can't eat two small parts after killing her at her flat.

Mervin, addict Durant added: "I ate what part of her I found eatable."

FULL STORY: PAGES 4 & 5

ADMISSION: Cannibal Paul Durant

TRAGIC: Karen's body was cut up

Paul Durant is led away in Spain; sections of his confession letter can be seen (inset).

Mark Hobson is revealed as a murderous cannibal in April 2005.

Cannibal who ate lover was on TV with him

THE MOMENT MR GAY UK CHOSE VICTIM

DEADLY SHOW
Morley was face-to-face with Damian on telly

Anthony Morley hit the headlines in October 2008 after it was revealed he killed his lover Damian Oldfield and proceeded to cook and eat some of his flesh.

▲ SICKENING Morley, left, cooked parts of victim Mr Oldfield

IAN KEY
iacy@mirror.co.uk

GAY cannibal killer Anthony Morley is seen with his future victim in a haunting TV scene.

Morley was on Big Brother host Davina McCall's late-night dating gameshow God's Gift in the mid-1990s.

He was seen performing a ball-strip in front of a studio audience of baying young males – one of whom was Damian Oldfield.

Morley, who won Mr Gay UK in 1993, faces life in jail after he was found guilty of murdering lover Mr Oldfield and eating part of him.

He will be sentenced on Monday for a crime described by the prosecution as "shocking and disturbing".

Chef Morley, 36, slashed his victim's throat in bed, sliced pieces of flesh from the body and cooked them in olive oil after seasoning them with parsley and other herbs, the jury heard.

He chewed part of the flesh and left other cooked pieces on his kitchen chopping board.

It was claimed it was an act of "punishment and revenge" because he could not deal with the fact that he was gay.

He carried out the sickening murder of gay magazine ads salesman Mr Oldfield, 33, after watching Brokeback Mountain with him in bed at home in Leeds.

He then went to a nearby takeaway and confessed to shocked staff and customers, claiming the other man was planning to rape him, Leeds crown court heard.

After the case, Detective Inspector Scott Wood of West Yorkshire Police said: "Thankfully, disturbing crimes of this type remain incredibly rare events."

Anthony Morley pictured during happier times as Mr Gay UK with Dannii Minogue.

Three of the victims of Stephen Griffiths, the self-proclaimed Crossbow Cannibal.

Eerily reminiscent of Dennis Nilsen, police were wondering whether there were bodies in the drains of Stephen Griffiths' house.

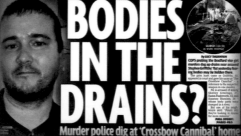

Police forensics search the area around Holmfield Court flats in Thornton Road, Bradford, home of Stephen Griffiths in May 2010.

Stephen Griffiths was being urged to admit his crimes in February 2011 when his health was deteriorating.

THE CANNIBAL GOES HOME .. BUT WHERE IS LOVER'S HEAD?

Porn star accused of butchering student back for murder quiz

Porn star Luka Magnotta was accused of butchering and eating Chinese student Jun Lin in 2012.

SWEENEY TODD GANG COOKED HUMAN PIES

Murdered women were baked

'CANNIBAL' COP

Jorge Silvetra was accused, with his wife and mistress, of murdering as many as nine women and baking them into pies in October 2012.

I'VE EATEN 2 WOMEN

Net boast to US cop on cannibal rap
British nurse arrest linked to horror

▲ TESTIFYING Valle's wife Kathleen

A BRITISH nurse has been arrested in connection with an American cop's alleged plot to kill and eat women.

Police were seen searching sheds at 57-year-old Dale Bolinger's house and digging in his garden.

Bolinger was held over alleged conspiracy offences connected to the cannibal cop, police confirmed.

Reports in the US claimed a British internet user - using the name MoodyBlues - boasted to New York cop Gilberto Valle he had eaten two people and gave him cannibalism tips.

Valle, 28, on trial in the United States for plotting to kidnap, cook and eat 100 women.

When Bolinger, of Canterbury, Kent, was asked about the alleged offences he replied: "Yes, I do deny them."

On February 21, he was also arrested separately over alleged grooming and possession of child abuse images.

MoodyBlues is said to have recommended eating a woman alive.

He said: "I think of it as eating her to death. The meat isn't quite like pork but very meaty."

He is also believed to have boasted how he had eaten a "black woman and a white person" and claimed to have a recipe for haggis using human offal.

Valle said he wasn't into raw meat and the men talked of severing a woman's feet and barbecuing them in front of her while she was alive.

Bolinger was questioned by Kent police in touch with US detectives hunting the British "mentor" of Valle.

MoodyBlues has not been identified in Manhattan Federal Court where Valle is on trial. US police told the court they believe the MoodyBlues comments were pure fantasy.

Mr Bolinger was questioned by police at home last Thursday, along with an unnamed 30-year-old man.

Bolinger is estranged from wife Kathleen, 55, who has cerebral palsy.

Yesterday Mr Bolinger's neighbours told how they saw police searching sheds and digging in his garden.

One said: "They were here the whole day. There were seven police vehicles.

"I could see police going into the back garden. There were two police dogs and they were looking through the two garden sheds.

"There was another police person with a shovel. I saw him digging all the soft soil in the flower beds. I think it was soil that looked like it had been dug up recently."

Mr Bolinger has been suspended from his job at Kent and Canterbury Hospital pending a police investigation.

A Kent Police spokeswoman said: "Two men aged 57 and 30 from the Canterbury area were arrested on February 21 over suspected conspiracy offences, grooming and possession of child abuse images. The two men are on police bail.

"Kent Police have been in touch with law enforcement authorities in the US in relation to this investigation.

"We can confirm it is in relation to the Gilberto Valle case in the US."

Valle, who discussed killing his wife Kathleen and other women denies charges of conspiracy to kidnap and improper use of a police computer.

- SUSPECT Bolinger denies the accusations yesterday

- DENIAL Valle says it's fantasy

Police were there all day ... I think it looked like recently dug up soil

'MoodyBlues' to the cop:

I think of it as eating her to death. The meat isn't quite like pork but very meaty. I also have a human recipe for haggis and foot is a favourite of mine

- RECIPE Bolinger accused of the advice

- DAD Valle with his daughter, is accused of horrific plot to rape and eat 100 women

---

'CANNIBAL' COP IS GUILTY

By ADRIAN SHAW

A NEW York cop linked with a British nurse to an alleged plan to kidnap and eat women was convicted yesterday of plotting to commit cannibalism.

Officer Gilberto Valle, 28, admitted he had a fetish for talking on the internet about eating human flesh.

His lawyers had urged the jury to ramblings of a fantasist but prosecutors said he had taken steps to abduct his wife and at least five other women.

New York's federal court heard he had looked up potential targets on a restricted database, researched chloroform and turned up near the home of one woman he had agreed to kidnap.

Prosecutor Hadassa Waxman said his interrupted a ghoulish plan to "kidnap, torture, rape and commit other horrific acts on young women".

Brit Dale Bolinger, 57, of Canterbury, Kent, was arrested last month after was revealed he allegedly boasted Bolinger, who remains on bail, said to have told Valle to eat a woman

---

The *Mirror* of 12th September 2013 shows British cannibal Geoffrey Portway and his torture dungeon.

Ouandja Magloire – nicknamed "Mad Dog" – is one of the most recent cannibals to hit the headlines in the trouble-hit Central African Republic, in January 2014.

this letter where he breaks that represents hope that we may find Karen's remains."

Later in October 2004, Durant's former landlady told how she feared she would be his next victim. Natalie Sanchez said the deranged killer terrorized her for days after he killed Karen. She said: "He was constantly phoning and trying to hunt me down." Before moving in with Karen, he had lived in Natalie's apartments in Calpe. She said: "I was sorry for him," but she felt uneasy at the same time. "He'd start crying – then break into laughter. One time I gave him a hug, but he started crushing me and I couldn't breathe." A few weeks later he had met Karen and Miles, and Natalie believed that he began plotting her murder from the start. He later showed her a mobile phone – probably Karen's – as well as a credit card in her name and the deeds to her home. Natalie reported him to police, who then discovered the grisly scene at Karen's apartment.

In June 2007, Durant went on trial for Karen's murder, and admitted manslaughter. Her body still hadn't been found. He also admitted to committing two murders in Britain. He was sentenced to 12 years in prison.

Mark Hobson

(2005)

Four-times killer Mark Hobson was revealed on 18th April 2005 to be a flesh-eating monster who had savagely murdered his girlfriend, her twin and an aged couple. A month before the murders, former bin man Hobson (35) had got probation and 100 hours' community work for stabbing William Brace (33), the former lover of a girl who jilted him, Samantha Batley. Mr Brace had life-saving surgery for five knife wounds. Amid astonishment after the verdict, the victim's mother said: "Where is the justice in that?"

Known to drink up to 36 cans of lager a day while taking drugs, Hobson inflicted 17 hammer blows on his girlfriend Claire Sanderson (27), Leeds Crown Court heard. With her body in the attic, he lured her twin, Diane, to their flat a week later. She was savagely beaten and had chunks of flesh bitten from her body. Hobson was thought to have eaten her left nipple. Diane suffered 15 minutes of torture, had her body shaved and was sexually mutilated – possibly while she was still alive. She was found at the flat in Camblesforth, North Yorkshire with severe injuries to her genital area. Hobson, who often beat Claire, had earlier told a work colleague he had "picked the wrong sister". He had a hit list which included the twins' parents and the mother and father of his ex-wife. But his third and fourth victims, slain a day after Diane died on 17th July 2004, were James Britton (80) and his wife Joan (81), at their home in Strensall, near York. Mr Britton, who had a Parkinson's-type disease, was stabbed several times and beaten with his own walking stick. His wife, who walked with a frame, was stabbed so viciously that the blade's wooden handle snapped off. Hobson was on the run for a week.

Hobson told police: "I'm a fucking murderer, aren't I? Then I'll take my punishment." The killer – cited as being obsessed with violent rap songs – admitted four murders, and the sentences were adjourned until May for reports.

James Britton was a former Spitfire pilot. He and his wife were attacked after Hobson had jumped bail. The killer pounced the moment Britton opened his door. James turned to flee, but Hobson repeatedly stabbed him in the back, then beat him with the walking stick as he lay dying in the hallway. When Joan found Hobson standing over her husband, a knife was plunged repeatedly into her body, puncturing several organs including her stomach and liver. The knife was left sticking out of her back when the handle finally snapped. The pair were found by a neighbour who visited every morning to check on them and take their clothes to be washed. One of their daughters, Catherine Wilkins (49), said: "Although my parents were elderly, he didn't have the right to say when and how they would die." Police, however, refused to link the murders to those of Claire and Diane until they had concrete evidence placing Hobson at the scene. The following day they got it, when scene-of-crime officers found three of his fingerprints on a door in the Brittons' home. More were found on a box that had been disturbed in the living room.

It transpired that Hobson had planned to wipe out Claire Sanderson's entire family after bludgeoning her to death in the frenzied hammer attack, as well as Ann and Terry Hales, his former wife Kay's parents. He lured Diane to his home after telling her that Claire was ill and wanted to see her; Diane had been worried that she hadn't heard from her sister. In notes found at his home by police, Hobson wrote how he wanted to sexually abuse and murder

Diane. He had battered Claire to death following a drinking session at a pub – police found no evidence of a sex attack. After she was lured to Hobson's home, Diane was hit on the head with a hammer, tied up and tortured. Hobson then took bites from her chest. She screamed so loudly that the killer stuck duct tape over her mouth and a plastic bag over her head. Even so, her piercing screams disturbed neighbours. Sarah Allen told police she had heard a woman's voice saying: "No, get off me." Stephen Atkinson had heard a man shout: "I'm not going to kill you." Then there was silence. Diane was severely sexually assaulted before she was smashed several times with a hammer and strangled. Her body was then dumped next to her sister's decomposing body.

Despite the murder, Hobson then met Diane's boyfriend, Ian Harrison, in a pub that night. He had earlier told Ian that the twins' dad had died, and that they were too upset to come out. Ian was even invited back to the flat where Claire and Diane had been murdered. He complained of a strange smell but was told it was the drains. Ian went to pay his respects the following day, but was shocked when the girls' father, George, opened the door. The pair went to Hobson's flat, opened the door with spare keys and were hit by the smell of rotting flesh. George found the mutilated bodies of his daughters. Hobson, was on the run.

Police launched a nationwide manhunt and Hobson was caught a week later thanks to his craving for cigarettes. Derek North (79) recognized Hobson when he visited his petrol station near Shipton, and phoned the police the moment he left. Armed officers arrived, and within minutes a tracker dog had found the killer in the corner of a field at the back of the garage. He offered no resistance, was handcuffed and led away. Hobson was thought to have been living rough before the police caught up with him.

Hobson's relationship with Claire had been volatile – he once pummelled her with his fists in front of a friend before dragging her 12 feet along the ground by her hair. Another friend had spotted bite marks on her shoulder. But Claire was besotted.

There was no clear motive for the murders, but friend Scott Shooter told of the killer's obsession with rap star Eminem – who had written a track about killing women. After his arrest, Hobson was held while detectives were given more time to question him. He spent two nights in hospital before the questioning began, and was charged with four murders on 29th July 2004 after nearly 60 hours of questioning. He first appeared before magistrates on the following day in Harrogate.

On 17th August 2004, Claire and Diane's parents joined 250 mourners to lay them to rest. Archdeacon of Doncaster Robert Fitzharris said that George and Jacqueline had faced a double horror in losing both their daughters. "To lose two children to murder is unimaginable," he said. Following the service Claire and Diane's coffins were taken from Holy Trinity church in Cowick, East Yorkshire to a private cremation.

In June 2005, it was announced that Hobson wanted to appeal against his "life means life" prison term. He had become the first prisoner in the UK who had admitted his crimes to receive a whole life sentence. He wanted, however, to be given credit for his guilty plea at Leeds Crown Court and to have the sentence reduced to a fixed term. The planned appeal was condemned by campaign groups. Clive Elliott of the Victims of Crime Trust said: "Hobson is a very real danger to society and should never be let free from prison. This is a clear demonstration of how murders not only destroy the lives of the victims, but also the families and communities affected by the crimes. It is the families of the victims who are left to suffer a life sentence as well, and life should indeed mean life for a killer. Rather than the courts focusing on what his apparent needs are, let us focus on the needs of the families of the victims and the communities which have been affected by the crimes."

Later, it was revealed that Hobson was begging women pen pals to send raunchy photographs to him in jail. "p.s. The more explicit the photo the better," he wrote. In a twisted love letter to one woman known as Alicia he bleated: "the media hasn't been showing the most flattering pictures of me". He went on that he was: "in a bit of a state at the moment, head wise", in a further bid for sympathy. He was said to have been a regular card player in Wakefield prison with double murderer Ian Huntley, but the pair fell out when Hobson accused the child-killer of welshing on a wager for an ounce of tobacco.

Cannibal Killer Jailed

(2005)

A cannibal killer who fed his gay lover victim's lungs to his cat was jailed for 13 years on 10th May 2005. Ralf Meyer (41) planned to devour teacher Joe Ritzowsky (33) himself after stabbing and cutting him up at his flat in Berlin, but he felt guilty for his "dark desires" after feeding the cat. He told police: "Stop me before I eat too."

Cannibal Jail Horror

(2007)

A prisoner killed a cellmate, then ripped open his chest and ate his lung, police said in January 2007. The attacker tore the man apart with his bare hands then yelled: "I've eaten his heart." A post mortem revealed a large part of the 41-year-old victim's lung and muscle had been devoured. Police then probed the gruesome remand cell attack at a prison in Rouen, northern France. A source said: "This is a terrifying act of cannibalism. We've never seen anything like this." The alleged attacker and a third cellmate were sent to solitary confinement.

In court, it was revealed that the cannibal convict had murdered and eaten his cellmate to "take over his soul". Nicolas Cocaign (39) attacked Thierry Baudry (41) after he gave him a "dirty look" in their shared cell. Cocaign then suffocated Baudry with a plastic bag before trying to cut out his heart with a pair of scissors. But he missed the heart and instead removed and ate the man's lung. He was charged with murder and acts of torture.

Cocaign was jailed for 30 years in June 2010 after being convicted of the heinous crime. Dubbed the Cannibal of Rouen, he told the French court that his appeals for psychological help had been ignored. He said: "I took action, they took me seriously."

In other news that same month, Yuri Vershkov (32) and Yuri Chupin (58) were jailed in Russia for 18 years for killing a friend, eating him and selling the leftovers to a kebab takeaway.

The Mauerova Family
(2007)

If it wasn't for a neighbour who picked up horrific images from the Mauerova family's baby monitor, because they owned the same make, it is unlikely that their crimes would have come to light quite so quickly.

The family from the Czech Republic were exposed as members of sinister religious cult the Grail Movement and cannibals following their neighbour's gruesome discovery. For eight months, unspeakable acts had been carried out on two young brothers, and relayed to the baby monitor so that the mother of the household could view them.

One eight-year-old boy, who was kept locked in a cellar, was skinned and his flesh was fed to relatives.

Klara Mauerova was seen weeping in court in June 2008 as the horrific details of the crimes were read out to the jury. She admitted torturing her son Ondrej and his brother Jakub (10). Both boys had been subjected to cigarette burns, attempted drownings and whippings on their bare flesh. The boys had also been sexually abused and forced to self-harm with knives, handcuffed so they couldn't escape and left standing in their own urine for days at a time.

The neighbour, from Brno, had installed a baby monitor so that he could keep a careful watch on his new-born child, but a signal from the identical monitor next door had showed one of his neighbour's boys naked, chained and being savagely beaten. Once police were called, three children, including the two brothers, were rescued from the property. The third "child" was eventually discovered to be Barbora Skrlova – later identified as one of the boys' abusers. Mauerova claimed that Skrlova and her own sister, Katerina, were behind the "sick" abuse. The court also heard how a man, known only as "Doctor", had sent the three women text messages with instructions on how to abuse the boys.

Klara Mauerova received just nine years for the torture, cannibalism and abuse of her own children. Katerina received a sentence of 10 years, while Skrlova – a tiny woman who was being groomed by the cult to take a leading role – was given five years' incarceration.

Özgür Dengiz
(2007)

On 5th June 2007, Turkish computer engineer Sedat Erzurumlu told Özgür Dengiz that he could not afford to buy the laptop he was interested in. Furious, Dengiz murdered Erzurumlu and three months later killed a worker at the Mamak Dump. A few hours after that, he murdered a municipal worker. He skinned the corpse of his last victim and ate some of the raw flesh, before leaving the body at the dump in bags. The flesh he took with him was deposited in his fridge at his home in Ankara, but was finally traced by police when he used one of the victim's mobile phones to make a number of calls. The flesh in the fridge was discovered by police and he was immediately arrested. He showed no emotion during his confession, and was convicted for his crimes and sentenced to a lengthy prison term. Cannibalism is taboo in Turkey, and the murderer's crimes caused an outcry from the public.

Jose Luis Calva
(2007)

When Alejandra Galeana disappeared in Mexico City in October 2007, police decided to question her partner Jose Luis Calva. As they entered his home they found Calva eating human flesh, and

Cannibal Killers

discovered the mutilated body of Alejandra in a cupboard. He tried to escape, but was soon captured after jumping from a window and injuring himself.

While violent crime has always been prevalent in Mexico City, even the most hardened of police officers were shocked at the depravity of Calva's murder and subsequent cannibalism. He was convicted and sentenced to more than 80 years in prison, and police suspected he was responsible for a further eight unsolved murders of young girls. Two months later, Calva committed suicide in his prison cell.

Anthony Morley
(2008)

A former Mr Gay UK killed a man for whom he had cooked dinner, and tried to eat his flesh, a jury heard on 6th October 2008. Ex-chef Anthony Morley was said to have seasoned bits of thigh with fresh herbs then fried them in olive oil. Police found six pieces of cooked flesh on a chopping board and a chewed piece in the kitchen bin.

Morley (36), the first Mr Gay UK in 1993 – denied murdering advertising salesman Damian Oldfield at his house in Leeds. He claimed the 33-year-old homosexual tried to rape him. Morley was said to have walked to a nearby takeaway in a bloodstained dressing gown and flip-flops. He asked staff to call the police, then sat outside waiting to be arrested. Mr Andrew Stubbs, QC, prosecuting, told the jury of eight women and four men at Leeds Crown Court that Morley was unsure of his sexuality, but he had arranged to meet Mr Oldfield, who worked for the publishers of a gay magazine called *Bent*, in Leeds in April.

They exchanged text messages earlier in the day, and in one of them Morley wrote: "Never been really properly gay. Tried being bi, tried being straight but never been a hundred per cent happy. Maybe one day I will find happiness." The pair later went back to Morley's house, where Morley made them both a meal. Afterwards they went up to his bedroom, where the alleged attack happened. Mr Oldfield had his throat cut while he was under the duvet and collapsed on the floor, where he was stabbed numerous times, including several times after he was already dead. Police found a nine-inch piece of skin and flesh, including a nipple, had been cut from his chest and left alongside the body, with a bank card put over the gaping wound. Another eight-inch slice was cut from his thigh. Mr Stubbs said that officers had found six pieces of cooked flesh on the chopping board. Saliva on the "chewed" flesh in the bin matched Morley's DNA profile. He allegedly told police: "Someone tried to rape me and I have killed that person." After his arrest, he was said to have mumbled: "I cooked him a nice meal. I said to take it slow, why did he do that?"

An ex-lover of the cannibal told the jury how Morley had once attacked him with a cleaver. It was only because he fell as he tried to strike Shaun Wood that he had missed. Moments later the attacker went upstairs and wrecked his bedroom, calling out: "I am psychotic, get me a doctor." Wood told the court: "It happened after he gave back some money I had loaned him." In the end police came and took Morley away. He was released the following day. The court was also told by Steven Robinson that he had been with Mr Oldfield in a Leeds bar a month before the killing. Morley had approached them and said: "I could kill with these hands."

On 18th October 2008, it was reported that Morley had been seen with his future victim on TV. Morley had been on Big Brother host Davina McCall's late-night dating gameshow God's Gift in the mid-1990s. He performed a half-strip in front of a studio audience of baying young males – one of whom was Damian Oldfield. By this time Morley had been found guilty of murdering Oldfield and eating part of his thigh. The crime was described by the prosecution as "shocking and disturbing" and an act of "punishment and revenge". After the case, Detective Inspector Scott Wood of West Yorkshire police said: "Thankfully, disturbing crimes of this type remain incredibly rare events."

Morley was jailed for life on 20th October 2008. He was told he would serve at least 30 years. Judge James Stewart, QC, told him: "This is one of the most gruesome murders I have encountered. I associated cannibalism with eras long gone, with the tale of Robinson Crusoe. No longer." There was applause from Leeds Crown Court when the convicted cannibal and murderer was sentenced.

Vince Weiguang Li

(2008)

Tim McLean (22) was riding on a Greyhound bus from Edmonton to Winnipeg, Canada, when he was attacked by Vince Weiguang Li on 30th July 2008. McLean had been sleeping, and passengers watched in horror when Li produced a knife and began stabbing the young man repeatedly in the neck and chest. The force of the unprovoked attack actually decapitated McLean. By this time the bus had come to a screeching halt, and passengers fled the vehicle as Li triumphantly held up the severed head of his victim.

As police raced to the scene west of Portage la Prairie on the Trans Canadian Highway, Li repeatedly returned to the body and took flesh from it, which he consumed in front of horrified witnesses. When the Royal Canadian Mounted Police arrived, Li was still on the bus while passengers were huddled at the roadside crying and vomiting. Five hours later, Li was apprehended by the police, who found more of the victim's flesh, including his ears and nose, in the murderer's pockets. The victim's eyes and slivers of his heart were eventually found to be missing. Li pleaded insanity in March 2009 and was sent to a secure psychiatric hospital.

Olesya Mostovschikova

(2009)

A woman killed a friend with an axe before cooking and eating her – in front of her seven-year-old son. Olesya Mostovschikova (27) told police that while drinking at home she quarrelled with her friend. She said: "With the axe I hit her on her head. I cut off her ears, gouged out one eye, cut off an arm and a hand and cooked them in the oven." The woman later sliced flesh from the victim's buttock, breast and a cheek, before cooking and eating it with another friend – whom she also threatened to kill. Police in Irkutsk, Russia were alerted after body parts were dumped in a bin.

Stephen Griffiths, the Crossbow Cannibal

(2010)

A man was questioned by detectives on 26th May 2010 after police launched a Yorkshire Ripper-style probe into the murders of three sex workers. The news sent shock waves through the red light district of Bradford, West Yorkshire, where Peter Sutcliffe killed some of his 13 victims in the Seventies. The three vice girls vanished from the same area while working the streets – one in June 2009, and two between April and May 2010. Police initially refused to link their disappearances, but later revealed that a man held on suspicion of the murder of Suzanne Blamires (36) – who vanished just a few days before the news broke – was also being quizzed about the disappearances of the other two. He was named as Stephen Griffiths (40), who lived in a flat on the outskirts of the city centre. Said to be a student of criminology specializing in homicide at Bradford University, he was arrested after body parts identified as Suzanne's were found in the River Aire at Shipley. A neighbour said that teetotaller Griffiths used to wander around in a long black leather coat and boast he was doing a "PhD in Jack the Ripper". It was also believed he had a social networking website under the name of an alleged alter ego, Ven Pariah. Police were granted extra time to question him over the missing women, Shelley Armitage (31) and Susan Rushworth (43), who had disappeared the previous year. At this point, the body in the river hadn't been identified, but it had been established that the remains were female.

An underwater unit continued to search a drainage culvert at the end of a cobbled street near the city centre, and forensic officers were seen checking black bin bags taken from rubbish skips behind university halls of residence. Shelley had last been seen on CCTV in Bradford's red light area; she and Suzanne knew each other and lived just a few streets apart. Shelley had drug and alcohol problems, but had been trying to clean up her lifestyle. Assistant Chief Constable Jawaid Akhtar confirmed that a man was being questioned over all three disappearances and West Yorkshire police were believed to be looking into other cases, including the disappearance of Gemma Simpson (23) in 2000 and Yvonne Fitt (33) in January 1992.

The student studying serial killers was charged with all three murders on 27th May 2010, and appeared in court the following day. Police were still hunting for Shelley's and Susan's bodies. Griffiths was described as a "model mature student" by Bradford University, where he had been studying patterns of crime in the city during the 19th century for six years. On his web page he described himself as a university researcher who was "single and straight". The page also featured pictures of him in a series of bizarre poses.

Forensic teams examined the flat where Suzanne had allegedly been killed. Police were said to have been alerted by a caretaker, following complaints about a disturbance. Suzanne, last seen a few days earlier, was believed to have met her attacker in the street and negotiated a £20 deal for sex. Her boyfriend reported her missing the following day, and bags containing her body parts were spotted by a walker close to the river bank. The black plastic bin liners were found to contain her torso and limbs; her head was found in a rucksack. Medical experts believed she had been battered and shot in the head with a crossbow before being dismembered.

Suzanne's mum, Nicky Blamires (54), paid a poignant tribute to her daughter. She said: "Unfortunately my daughter went down the wrong path and she didn't have the life she was meant to have. She was a much-loved daughter and what has happened will haunt me to the day I die. She always knew that she could come home. The door was always open. We saw her all the time and were there for her. At the end of the day nobody deserves this. All these girls were human beings and people's daughters."

A distraught ex-vice girl who was close friends with the three murdered women said that each of them had been desperately trying to turn their lives around and get off the streets. Anna Kennedy (36) described Suzanne, Shelley and Susan as "beautiful friends". She added: "All those girls who died were my friends and I could have been next. This terrifies me and I feel sick when I think how close I came. It could have been me." Anna, who was a sex worker for 13 years, was helping vice girls to start a new life away from the grim streets of the city's red light area. All three women who died had taken her advice to heart and were striving for a new beginning, away from prostitution and drugs. Anna had seen Susan on the day she vanished, and had been delighted to find her planning to give up vice for the sake of her three children. Susan was also beating the heroin addiction that had forced her there in the first place. Anna added: "Susan loved her children to bits. She had really cleaned up and turned her life around just for them. I was with her the day she disappeared and we had a chat outside Costa Coffee. She was with her mum who she had moved back in with." Shelley was also determined to start again and planned to start a family. Anna said: "Shelley had a heart of gold and a beautiful smile. She would do anything for anyone. She was trying for a baby with her childhood sweetheart. They had been together since she was about 15." Anna had seen Suzanne two days before she disappeared. They chatted at a mission which helped vice girls where Anna worked as a volunteer. She said: "I saw Amber, that's her street name, at the mission on the Wednesday before she vanished. I could not believe it when I heard she had disappeared. I used to stay at her flat; we were good friends."

Police said that Susan had never gone missing before, and they were concerned because she did not have her medication for epilepsy with her. After three weeks, they had grave concerns for her welfare, and it was feared she might have died from an overdose of a particularly potent batch of heroin that had killed several other users. However, her son James said: "She had been off heroin for five weeks before she went missing and was getting help for her addiction. There is no reason she'd have just left. She'd recently started seeing her grandchildren and was getting to know them." Friends said that Shelley's disappearance was also unexpected, as she had recently bought a puppy which she adored and hated to be parted from. A woman who lived next door to Suzanne for 10 years said she had been forced into prostitution by an abusive boyfriend. She added: "He sent her to her death. He has blood on his hands. He forced her out on to the street to pay for his drugs … if she didn't bring enough money back he would beat her up and drag her around by her hair. She went through hell, that poor girl." The friend spoke as she laid flowers at the address where Suzanne had previously lived. She had been fined in 2001 for propositioning a plain clothes officer in the area around the university, and the vice squad had stepped up patrols near halls of residence, fearing sex workers were moving there from the red light area. Superintendent Angela Williams said: "The vice team know all three girls very well and are distressed. Our officers try to intervene and put them in touch with agencies. Some have even given up days off to help them decorate their homes."

At the end of May 2010, the drains near the accused's home were dug by police, who feared that bodies could be hidden there. The grim hunt came as Griffiths appeared in court and gave his name as "The Crossbow Cannibal" – a reference to the murder weapon. He stood accused of crimes that ranked among Britain's most gruesome in decades, yet his court appearance turned into a macabre piece of theatre. As he gave his name, some of the missing women's relatives gasped and sobbed. There was a further surprise moment when Griffiths was asked for his address, and he said: "Erm, here, I guess." He appeared composed from the moment he strode into Courtroom 3 of Bradford Magistrates' Court for the three-minute hearing. At first he walked the wrong way into the glass-fronted dock and was guided to the correct position by an officer. As he stood, flanked by three security guards, he clasped his hands together as if in prayer. On several occasions he stroked his hair, then looked down, fidgeted and picked at his fingers as the court clerk read out the three murder charges. He was represented by solicitor Phillip Ainge, who worked for the law firm whose founder Kerry Macgill had represented Peter Sutcliffe: Griffiths had specifically asked for the firm Lumb and Macgill.

It was revealed at this time that police searching for missing chef Claudia Lawrence were known to be talking to the officers who had arrested Griffiths to see if there was a link. The York University worker had vanished in March 2009, and detectives wanted to establish if their colleagues' investigation could shed any light on the case. North Yorkshire police confirmed they would be liaising closely with the West Yorkshire force. Claudia (36) had vanished after leaving her York home. She had told a friend she had been out with a mystery boyfriend the day before she vanished, and the man had never been traced.

Meanwhile, as police continued their hunt in the drains, one resident said: "They told me they are looking in the drains to see if they can find remains." Utility firms had dug up the roads in the previous few weeks, and detectives wanted to find out if anything relating to the murders was dumped in the ditches. They were also searching a fast-flowing river just 400 yards from Griffiths' flat. A dozen wreaths lay outside the flats. One said: "For our special daughter Shelley Marie, goodnight, God bless your ever loving mum and dad."

Griffiths' father said that he and his son were estranged. Mr Griffiths, who had just returned from a family holiday, said: "He left home over 22 years ago, before he was 19. I haven't seen or spoken to him in going on 10 years and at first I didn't recognize that picture … He's changed a lot. All our sympathies are with the victims and their families." A police source said: "The search will go on for as long as it needs to go on. It is only right and proper that we check every lead to find the two missing women for the sake of their relatives." Officers were still combing through the killer's flat and it was reported that they were likely to closely examine the maps on his wall and his academic books about serial killers. At his second court appearance at the Crown Court Griffiths was more restrained, spending most of the hearing staring down at his hands, which were clasped in his lap. But as 18 relatives of the missing women strained to get a closer look at him, on several occasions he stared back at them. The judge agreed he could appear via video link for his next court hearing on 7th June – and he was then driven back to Wakefield prison.

Police were concentrating their investigation on 128 sites around Bradford as they hunted for remains. Forensic experts continued their search in the River Aire, but they also carried out searches across the city centre, sweeping the streets for clues and taking samples of drainwater. Wasteland behind the block of flats where Griffiths lived was also cleared of shrubs and scrutinized in minute detail. The massive operation was expected to take weeks. Police had already found a bag containing knives and hacksaws at the bottom of the River Aire, just a few yards from where the body parts had been found. The black canvas bag also appeared to contain fragments of human flesh. More human tissue was thought to have been found in the river, near where the bag was found. Detectives believed the tools might have been a macabre "killing kit" that had been used to dismember the bodies of all three women. Once the bag had dried out it was checked for fingerprints and DNA. Suzanne's killing was said to have been captured on CCTV and police had recovered nearly all her dismembered body parts. Meanwhile, police were trying to track down Griffiths' mother, Moira (61), who had not been seen since her son's arrest. Police said they urgently wanted to speak to her, but had been unable to find her. Her mobile had been switched off all week. Her neighbours described her as "kind and caring" and said she would be devastated that her son had been charged with such evil crimes. The city's vice girls left a floral tribute to the victims with the following words:

We'll often lie awake at night when others are asleep.
We'll take a walk down memory lane with tears upon our cheek.
No one will know the heartache we'll try so much to hide.
No one will know how many times we've broken down and cried.
We shared happy times, sad ones too.
The saddest day of all our lives is the day we lost you ...

Locals confirmed that they referred to Griffiths – an ex-public schoolboy – as "Lizard Man". He was given the nickname because he walked two pet Monitor lizards on leads and took them to nightclubs. Police had not recovered the meat-eating lizards.

Griffiths' family was devastated by the events. His uncle, Joe Dewhirst, said: "This has hit us hard. The entire family has been traumatized. We don't know what to make of it all."

At the beginning of June, it was revealed that police were probing links with two unsolved killings in Sheffield's red light district, 50 miles away. Michaela Hague (25) had gone missing in 2001 and Dawn Shields (19) in 1994. Griffiths was known to regularly visit Sheffield, and one Bradford sex worker said that he once suggested he should take her there because she would make more money. She added: "He even offered to keep an eye on me." Despite the widespread searches, further remains still hadn't been found back in Bradford. It was thought that Griffiths would be questioned again by police. Officers were trawling through his extensive paperwork, scores of books about serial killers and historical murders as well as a biography of Saddam Hussein, and a vast collection of DVDs that had been found at his home – his crossbow and bolts had already been recovered in a converted mill. Griffiths had ordered the crossbow parts earlier in 2010 from Amazon. Police were also analysing his website, which included pictures of more than 50 serial killers.

In early June, it was announced that the remains of Shelley had been found by police. The papers also revealed that Griffiths had two connections with two other convicted killers. It transpired that he had attended the same public school – Queen Elizabeth Grammar School in Wakefield – as serial killer John George Haigh, and that the convicted murderer Kenneth Valentine had lived in the flat above him. Valentine had strangled sex worker Caroline Creevy (25) in his flat in 1996. He had then dumped her body in a storm drain; it was later found by frogmen. After his conviction, the flats in Bradford's red light district were renamed Holmfield Court. In 1991, Valentine had been convicted of killing Janet Willoughby from Leeds after sexually assaulting her. He was cleared of murder, but found guilty of manslaughter and served five years of his seven-year sentence.

Meanwhile, Griffiths' mother Moira broke her silence over her

Cannibal Killers

son's crimes. She said: "It makes me feel horrible just thinking about it. I'm in shock."

For most of the 23-minute hearing at Bradford Crown Court, in which Griffiths appeared via video link from Wakefield prison, he sat with his eyes closed and at one point appeared to be asleep. He kept his head down and held a piece of paper in his hands. A provisional trial date was set for 16th November by Judge James Goss, QC. It was thought that Griffiths would be moved to a secure hospital for psychiatric assessment.

Two days later, Griffiths failed in a suicide attempt. He tried to suffocate himself by tying a sock around his neck and putting a plastic bag over his head. It was believed he briefly lost consciousness before prison officers found him slumped in his cell. Griffiths was transferred to a prison hospital. A prison source said "he failed miserably", and had tried to take the coward's way out. By this time, detectives were investigating whether Griffiths had actually eaten part of Suzanne's body after he chopped it into pieces. It was reported that psychiatrists were to be asked to assess whether the alleged killer should be moved to Rampton Hospital because of mental health concerns.

Kirsty Rushworth (21) sat in the packed courtroom on 15th October, able to see in person the man accused of murdering her mother. Griffiths did not look towards the young woman at any point, but sat with his head down and arms folded for the 25-minute hearing at Bradford Crown Court. He spoke only once to answer his name. His case was adjourned until 21st December 2010, when he was expected to appear at Leeds Crown Court.

Griffiths attempted suicide again on 19th November by swallowing batteries and pills. He was rushed to hospital from Wakefield jail and was expected to undergo emergency surgery to remove four batteries. He had been remanded in Ian Huntley's old cell on the medical wing of the prison. He was also placed on suicide watch while in his hospital bed at Pinderfield Hospital. An insider said: "If the battery acid leaks it can kill you and they don't know as yet what tablets he took so they may have to operate." If he didn't need surgery he was expected to be back in prison "within hours". Griffiths' overdose had been witnessed by prison officers. A source said: "He took the pills at tea time and was also seen swallowing the batteries." The insider added: "He tried to kill himself just weeks ago by cutting his throat. He has told inmates that he doesn't want to stand trial and has been causing a lot of trouble."

After his fourth suicide bid on 21st November, Griffiths was once again taken back to prison. It was said that he was desperate to be transferred to Rampton. Keeping him on suicide watch was costing taxpayers £1,688 a day. Four prison guards were paid overtime at £17.59 an hour to cover shifts. Being in Huntley's cell wasn't helping – inmates were telling Griffiths that it was cursed, and an insider said: "He wants out … All the staff are on overtime as it means checking the camera round the clock. If he goes out of the cell, it needs four staff to keep an eye on him. Two prison staff on each 12-hour shift watch him." Griffiths would certainly have had better conditions at Rampton Hospital, but jail chiefs rejected his plea.

In early February 2011 the *Mirror*'s Jeremy Armstrong wrote: "He was once muscular, fit and stocky. Now he is gaunt and frail, weighing barely 7st as he slowly starves himself to death in a prison hunger strike." He continued: "And though few will mourn the passing of self-styled Crossbow Cannibal Stephen Griffiths, he has no shortage of visitors."

Teams of detectives had spent hours at Griffiths' bedside, hoping to hear him whisper the terrible secrets of his grisly murder spree before he took them to the grave. They wanted the former criminology student to make a deathbed confession detailing all his crimes – to bring peace of mind to the distraught families of at least seven other women who went missing, and whom he could have slaughtered. By this time Griffiths was serving three life sentences for the murders of Suzanne, Susan and Shelley. He had cut up all three victims and claimed he had eaten parts of their flesh. He was pictured on CCTV clutching a crossbow and giving a defiant one-fingered gesture after killing one of the women.

In February, Griffiths was entering yet another month of hunger strike, and police wanted to question him about a string of other unsolved cases. Detectives made daily trips to his cell in Wakefield jail's hospital wing in a desperate effort to get him to talk, while three guards remained on duty outside at all times. Two murder squad officers spent two hours at his bedside at the beginning of the month; another two returned for two hours later that same afternoon. Finally, as darkness fell, two more arrived to spend the evening with the murderer, by this point a wizened and hunched figure.

A source said: "They have always known that he may have killed many more women, including prostitutes. They are looking at a long list of unsolved crimes and disappearances, especially in the Yorkshire area – and because of his worsening health time is rapidly running out." Griffiths was reported to be so weak he could no longer haul himself out of bed or sit up properly, and he had to be moved around in a wheelchair. He was said to be surviving on an occasional cup of water and fruit cordial. The prison chaplain called every day to offer spiritual guidance – but Griffiths kept telling him to "get lost". So far, he had stubbornly refused to co-operate with police. He had also made a living will, which meant that if his heart failed, prison doctors were forbidden to try to resuscitate him. Psychologists had decided he was sane – so he had been allowed to continue his hunger strike. A prison source said: "At one time it would have been classed as self-harm, but not any more. Apparently he is within his rights."

Griffiths had boasted after his arrest that he was a prolific serial killer and taunted police that there were many more victims they did not know about. He was obsessed with the Yorkshire Ripper, Peter Sutcliffe, and the unsolved cases that were ascribed to him focused mainly on Bradford, where many of Sutcliffe's horrific crimes were committed, and Sheffield, where Sutcliffe was finally caught.

Griffiths was told it was his last chance to clear his conscience, but privately some senior officers were convinced he just didn't care. He had told detectives shortly after his arrest: "This is the end of the line for me. I've killed a lot more than Suzanne Blamires. I've killed loads." He added: "Peter Sutcliffe came a cropper in Sheffield. So did I – but at least I got out of the city." Prison staff regularly checked his body with a metal detector after the battery incident, and warders were told to contact detectives immediately if he showed any signs of wanting to make a last confession. They were also ordered to address him respectfully as "Mr Griffiths" or "Stephen Griffiths".

Paul Thompson, the heartbroken brother of victim Susan Rushworth, spoke about the torment of not knowing what Griffiths did with her body. He said: "Until we know what happened we cannot properly grieve for her." He added bitterly: "I don't want Stephen Griffiths to die – I want him to stay trapped in his own private hell."

Griffiths had told police that he had killed six times. Police were probing unsolved cases, including that of Rebecca Hall (19), who had been battered to death in Bradford in April 2001. Her body was dumped in an alley just yards from Griffiths' flat. Yvonne Fitt had been found bound and gagged in a shallow grave after going missing, and Gemma Simpson was still missing. Michaela Hague had been killed on Bonfire Night 2001 in a Sheffield car park used by sex workers after she was picked up by a man in a blue Ford Sierra. Dawn Shields had been strangled and buried in a shallow grave at Mam Tor, Derbyshire in 1994.

It has been said that Griffiths was obsessed with Kenneth Valentine, but that he beat the older man badly when he discovered that he had killed. Some said that the men were so close that there was a possibility they had become lovers. Despite hating what Valentine had done, Griffiths was fascinated. He had already been to prison for three years at the age of 17 for an unprovoked knife attack on the manager of a supermarket, and was known to have told police at the time that he wanted to become a serial killer. Police were suspicious of Griffiths before the three murders and had already removed quite an arsenal of weapons, particularly hunting weapons, from his flat. Psychiatrists had warned he was obsessed with serial killers, while he was also obsessed with crime films – and even stated on his website that he would kill.

Griffiths dismembered all three victims in the bath at his flat. Susan was linked to the crime scene by a trace amount of blood – police believed she had been battered with a hammer. Only a few body parts of Shelley were ever found – but video footage of her showed up on Griffiths' mobile phone, which he had sold on; it was handed in to police. CCTV footage of Griffiths killing Suzanne was the main evidence against him. She was seen captured on camera fleeing from his flat before he chased her, wrestled with her, punched her and knocked her unconscious. Griffiths then shot her twice, in cold blood, in the head with a crossbow. He was captured by the same CCTV camera later that night leaving his flat with bin liners – the ones that police found in the river. Police confirmed in due course that other video footage and the body parts which were later found proved that Griffiths had skinned and then eaten parts of his victims' flesh.

Griffiths gave up his hunger strike after 120 days, and the warped "Crossbow Cannibal" announced that he was going to sue prison bosses for "failing" to look after him. A source said: "Griffiths thinks he can sue the prison service for failure in their duty of care.

You could not make it up. He claims his strike was to see how newspapers and TV covered his possible death. He claims he only wanted to know how far he could go and see how his victims felt. He thinks he has set a new hunger strike record. He looks like a concentration camp survivor."

Having been sentenced to a whole life tariff, Stephen Griffiths remains in prison today.

Matej Curko
(2011)

The "Slovak Cannibal" hunted on the grounds of the internet, and following his arrest and subsequent death, police believed he had carried out more than 30 murders. The cannibal was eventually caught when police were alerted by a Swiss man who had met the killer in a chatroom. The man told police that Curko had tried to coerce him into cannibalism and suicide.

Police traced the married father of two to his home village of Sokol in Slovakia in the summer of 2011. Going undercover, they lured Curko to meet an officer, but when they arrived on the scene, the murderer produced a gun and was shot by a police sniper. When his home was searched, officers found a very large collection of body parts, including those belonging to two Slovakian women who had disappeared the previous year. It was believed that the women had readily agreed to take part in Curko's "sick" fantasies.

While friends and neighbours were completely shocked when Curko was identified as a cannibal, it seems that he was one of a new breed of internet predators, who prey on vulnerable victims to fuel their cannibalistic desires.

Michael Schneider
(2011)

A banker's head was found "bobbing" in a stewpot in the flat of a suspected cannibal killer. Body parts of Carsten Schmidt (37) were wrapped in baking foil and strewn across the Berlin flat. Police claimed: "It was a horror show." Michael Schneider (42), who was said to have tried to kill himself at the scene, was charged with murder.

Cannibalized German Tourist
(2011)

A cannibal killer suspected of eating a round-the-world yachtsman was being hunted by police in October 2011. Guide Henri Haiti was believed to have killed German Stefan Ramin (40) and eaten him. Stefan's remains were discovered in the embers of a campfire on the island of Nuku Hiva in the Pacific Ocean.

The yachtsman's girlfriend, Heike Dorsch (37), said she escaped from the guide after he had chained her to a tree and sexually assaulted her. Stefan, a former business adviser from Haselau in northern Germany, was on a worldwide sailing tour with Heike when they visited the French Polynesian island. Reports in Germany said they stopped off at Nuku Hiva in their catamaran on 16th September, and Stefan went missing when he went on a goat hunt with Haiti. Heike went looking for him after the guide told her: "There's been an accident. He needs help." But instead of helping her find Stefan, he was said to have taken her captive and put her through a sex ordeal. Hours later, she managed to escape and alerted the authorities.

Stefan had been missing for a week when the police found his remains in a remote valley. Bones, teeth and melted fillings were also found in the campfire ashes. *Moby Dick* author Herman Melville claimed he was once captured by a tribe of cannibals on Nuku Hiva. He escaped before they could eat him.

Isakin Jonsson and the "Vampire Girl"

(2012)

A Satan-worshipping vampire and a cannibal asked for permission to marry behind bars in February 2012. Isakin Jonsson (33) had cut off an ex-girlfriend's head and eaten her body parts, while Michelle Gustafsson (23) had stabbed a man to death and drunk his blood.

The engaged killers, who boasted of their crimes on the internet, were both receiving psychiatric treatment at a high-security facility near Katrineholm in Sweden. It was said that neither were ever likely to be let out. Gustafsson posted online: "We want to live together, have dogs and pursue our hobbies – piercing and tattoos." Jonsson said: "I love Michelle. I have never met anyone like her." At the time, officials refused to answer whether they would agree to the couple's request.

Alexander Bychkov
(2012)

A cannibal killer admitted to eating the livers of at least six victims in March 2012. Alexander Bychkov (24) confessed as police quizzed him about a minor theft. Police in Penza, southern Russia said: "He suddenly admitted killing and eating half a dozen people." In another case, a 35-year-old man confessed to killing his friend and selling his meat as "pork" in Vladivostok. Meanwhile, Bychkov – who called himself "Rambo" – admitted he also ate the hearts of two of his victims.

Bychkov was jailed for life on 22nd March 2013, having been found guilty of killing and butchering nine homeless and alcoholic men using a knife and a hammer. He confessed to murdering one and cutting him up after a drinking session. He said: "I only took his heart. Two days later I cooked and ate it." Police found a diary detailing the killings as well as violent films, books and newspaper clippings about mass killers. One of Bychkov's victims was said to be his mother's ex-boyfriend. All she could say was: "I can't believe my son has killed anyone." Meanwhile, it transpired that the motive for the crimes was to impress his girlfriend, who had dumped him just before the murders were carried out.

The victims' remains were all found buried near the killer's home and in the city's dump.

Charles Taylor
(2012)

Former Liberian dictator Charles Taylor was found guilty, on 26th April 2012, of sponsoring a brutal civil war that left tens of thousands dead. Taylor, the first head of state to be convicted by an international court since the Second World War, was to serve his sentence in a British jail at a cost of around £100,000 a year. Witnesses said his soldiers were cannibals, and he too was accused of eating human flesh. Taylor (64) was found guilty of 11 charges of aiding war crimes – including terror, murder, rape and conscripting child soldiers – though he was cleared of having direct control over the troops he supported.

Taylor provided arms for rebels who were fighting in neighbouring Sierra Leone during its civil war, which took place between 1991 and 2002. The guerrillas gave him diamonds, known as blood diamonds because they were mined by slave labourers in war zones and sold to finance armies. Taylor showed no emotion as the verdict was handed down. Presiding judge Richard Lussick said the prosecution had proved beyond reasonable doubt that Taylor was "criminally responsible" for aiding and abetting crimes by rebels in Sierra Leone.

The judge said the accused had sold diamonds and bought weapons on behalf of the rebels, and knew they were committing atrocities. Prosecutor Brenda Hollis said: "Today is for the people of Sierra Leone who suffered horribly at the hands of Taylor and his proxy forces. The judgment brings some justice to the many thousands of victims who paid a terrible price for Mr Taylor's crimes. The conviction sends a powerful message that even those in the highest positions can be held to account for grave crimes." Elise Keppler, senior counsel for Human Rights Watch, said: "Not since Nuremberg has an international or hybrid war crimes court issued a judgment against a current or former head of state."

Supermodel Naomi Campbell had appeared at the five-year trial in The Hague at a UN-backed special court. She gave evidence alleging that Taylor had given her three diamonds after a dinner hosted by Nelson Mandela in 1997. She told the court in 2010 that she received three "small, dirty-looking stones" but had no idea who sent them. Actress Mia Farrow, who was also at the meal in South Africa, testified that Ms Campbell told her that Taylor had sent his men to present her with a "huge diamond", and that she intended to hand it to Mr Mandela's charity. This evidence went to the heart of the case.

Judges heard gruesome testimony from victims of the Sierra Leone conflict. One witness said he had seen the Liberian leader eat human liver. Taylor denied the allegation, and called the trial a "sham".

Warlord Taylor was elected president in 1997 after terrorizing people to vote for him, and was forced to resign in 2003. He was set to serve his sentence in Britain because the Dutch had agreed only to host the trial. British Foreign Secretary William Hague said the verdict was a warning to Syria's president Bashar al-Assad, who was also accused of human rights abuses. "Dawn of justice has finally come" wrote the *Mirror* on 27th April 2012: "Sierra Leone's brutal and bloody civil war was fuelled by a lust for diamonds. Rebels forced child soldiers to fight and gave them drugs to desensitize them from the horrors they were committing. Beheadings, disembowellings and amputations were common. Up to 500,000 people were killed, mutilated or raped and many were made to work in mines. Arms were smuggled from Liberia in sacks of rice and diamonds were sent back in mayonnaise jars, with Taylor once receiving a 45-carat and two 25-carat stones. Student Halimatu Jalloh, 27, whose sister was raped and killed, celebrated Taylor's conviction in Sierra Leone's capital, Freetown. Her hand-painted sign said: 'Orphans, widows, widowers, rape victims, amputees and all the war affected, wipe your tears as the dawn of justice has come.'"

On 30th May 2012 Charles Taylor was sentenced to 50 years in prison.

Hans Rudel

(2012)

A politician who offered his friend's wife and daughter to cannibals –
to save his friend from a messy divorce – was jailed for seven years
in May 2012. Hans Rudel had placed an internet ad pretending to
be the woman and her 12-year-old daughter looking for a "strict
master" to "roast them on a spit". Rudel (53) was caught when
an undercover police officer responded to the advertisement. The
S&M fanatic, of Winterhur, Switzerland, said he wanted to help Peter
Joachim (50) who had split from Patricia (27). He told a Swiss court:
"I was hoping Patricia would be picked up by a butcher and never
appear again." Rudel, founder of a local BDP conservative party
branch, had already served 10 years for murdering a young woman
and impaling her on a tree in 1988.

Luka Rocco Magnotta

(2012)

A porn star filmed himself hacking a man to death with an ice pick,
then posted the victim's dismembered body parts to political parties.
Luka Rocco Magnotta sent the victim's foot to Canada's Conservative
Prime Minister Stephen Harper and a hand to the Liberals. Police had
launched their hunt for the 29-year-old maniac, who had previously

posted gruesome footage online of himself torturing and killing kittens, after the mutilated torso of Magnotta's victim was found stuffed inside a suitcase behind a block of flats in Montreal. Shocked police chief Ian Lafreniere said it was the worst crime scene his force had ever come across: "As a father, I would have trouble sleeping at night knowing that the suspect was in my neighbourhood. This is the kind of crime scene my officers have never seen."

Magnotta's sickening 11-minute snuff video, titled "1 Lunatic 1 Ice Pick", was posted on a Canadian website. It purports to show the bisexual killer attacking an Asian man who is tied to a metal bed. He chops him up while 'True Faith' by New Order plays in the background.

Hours after the victim's torso was found, a blood-stained package containing a foot arrived at the offices of the Conservative Party in Ottawa. A horrified adviser to the PM discovered the rotting limb. Party spokesman Fred DeLorey said: "It was such a horrible odour, many of us will not forget it." At around the same time a postal worker discovered a hand inside a package addressed to the Liberal Party of Canada. Police, who believed Magnotta could have fled abroad, feared that more body parts would be discovered in the following days. Mr Lafreniere said: "We're still missing parts of the body so it's difficult for us at this time to identify the man 100 per cent." The officer said that police had successfully removed the video from the internet earlier in the week, but that it kept reappearing. He added: "It's horrible. I can't believe people take advantage of watching this."

Police investigating the gruesome case named the victim as the murder suspect's lover – Chinese student Jun Lin (33), who had been reported missing. Meanwhile, it was revealed that a clubber had unwittingly spent two nights with the fugitive cannibal killer after picking him up in a gay nightclub in Paris – where police believed he would be found. The man told police he only found out who his guest had been after spotting the porn actor's photo on the Web when he left. The traumatized man immediately told detectives, and a police source said: "After he left, the man realized who he had had staying and contacted us. It is then thought he went out drinking in the Bastille district and was staying in a cheaper hotel in the east of the city." An international manhunt was underway for Magnotta, who had also eaten his victim's body parts.

Canadian police believed that Magnotta could be disguised as a woman, and had received "credible information" from eyewitnesses who claimed to have spotted the fugitive. French daily newspaper *Le Parisien* said that one bar owner told police: "He came into my bar and sat drinking and chatting. He seemed very excited." A receptionist at a hotel near the Champs-Elysees revealed he stayed there the same night. Canadian police launched a cold case review, on suspicion that Magnotta could be a serial killer who had murdered many times. He had once boasted in an email: "Once you kill, and taste blood, it's impossible to stop. The urge is just too strong."

Interpol had notified authorities in 190 countries to be on the lookout for the Canadian murderer, and he was arrested in a Berlin internet café by armed police on 4th June 2012. Eyewitnesses said the porn actor was reading about the murder case online when officers brandishing weapons pinned him to the floor and cuffed him. "Are you the wanted man?" an officer asked. "Yes, that's me," said Magnotta. He offered no resistance.

Police revealed that they had tracked Magnotta to Paris via his mobile phone. He had been seen getting on the overnight bus to Berlin at the Bagnolet international bus station in Paris; the Eurolines bus company handed over bus station CCTV footage and paperwork to police. The hunt ended in the café – in the Neukoelln gay district – when a customer recognized him from media coverage and called the police. The keen computer gamer was arrested and Canadian embassy officials were informed. Extradition proceedings started immediately, so that he could be sent home within a fortnight to face charges of murder as well as charges of threatening Canada's prime minister.

Magnotta, who also used the names Eric Clinton Newman and Vladimir Romanov, had worked as a rent boy under the name Angel. Online postings, believed to have been his work, included a short animation that involved a bloody handprint and the phrase "It was Luka Magnotta". He posted numerous images of himself, including one with the message, "I'm not bad, I'm just drawn that way," the catchphrase of cartoon femme fatale Jessica Rabbit from the 1988 film *Who Framed Roger Rabbit?* Over the years he had undergone plastic surgery, frequently worn make-up and dyed his hair to change his appearance. He had also disguised himself as a woman. Police in Germany believed he had been trying to get to Eastern Europe, where he could have remained on the run.

Magnotta did not fight extradition charges from Europe and a judge remanded him in custody accused of murder. Police said after the hearing: "According to statements to lawyers, he won't fight extradition."

Meanwhile, two schools in Vancouver received body parts which were believed to be from murder victim Jun Lin. Vancouver police said the parcels came from Montreal and were accompanied by notes, but they refused to release any further details in case of copycat killers.

On 9th June 2012, writing in the *Mirror*, Annette Witheridge said: "Youngster Eric Newman smiles innocently into the camera for his school yearbook picture. Back then, in 1993 he was a painfully shy 11-year-old who retreated into a fantasy world to forget his nightmarish home life." In a bid to impress his disbelieving classmates, he spun incredibly outlandish tales – something he continued to do long after he left school.

Witheridge writes: "As an adult, he'd lie about being the lover of Canada's most notorious female killer. Today, however, Eric stands accused of something which truly defies belief. For he grew up to become Luka Magnotta ... arrested over a cannibal slaying. According to police, he killed and mutilated gay lover Jun Lin, then ate his flesh with a knife and fork. He also filmed it all and later posted the sick video online ...

"Investigators are trying to unravel his sick fantasy world, which began in the Toronto suburbs where Eric grew up – and also spread to Wembley, North London. His upbringing was certainly brutal – at least one of his relatives always suspected there was something seriously wrong. An aunt, who asked not to be identified, said: 'He is a nut job – he was a time bomb waiting to explode.' His parents – Anna Yourkin and Donald Newman – were just teenagers when he was born and they split up soon after. Eric was then brought up mainly by his domineering granny Phyllis Yourkin. Beatings were common and Eric – the eldest of three – took the brunt of his grandmother's temper. Out of his home, he wanted to fit in at Charlottetown Junior School in the sprawling Toronto suburb of Scarborough.

"But the few classmates who remember him say they used to laugh at the tall tales he told. The spotty, blue-eyed boy even tried to make Eric, his old-fashioned first name, more glamorous. He claimed his mother had named him after Hollywood star Julia Roberts' actor brother Eric. It was a strange claim – because Julia and Eric's careers had not taken off when he was born.

"When caught out by his lies, there were flashes of violent temper – at 12 he hurled a chair at a teacher. As he entered his teens he had overly effeminate mannerisms – and boasted about his sexual conquests. Around the same time, he left Toronto and moved with his granny to Lindsay, Ontario. His classmates at IE Weldon Secondary School remembered him as a kid who constantly switched his hair colour from jet-black to peroxide blond. But his aunt feared for his mental health. 'I didn't trust him,' she said. 'He is mentally ill. He has delusions of grandeur. He concocts stories and they, in turn, become fact in his mind.'"

Detectives investigating the gruesome death of Lin were

desperately trying to unravel the internet boasts of Magnotta to see if he had killed before. Mr Lafreniere said: "We are looking at an unsolved murder, but our problem is the fiction. Everyone would love to link him to every unsolved murder in North America because like your Jack the Ripper he has made taunts about what he has done." Police then created a timeline to see if they could place the murderer at any other murder scenes. Mr Lafreniere said: "It is a horrible task because he travelled everywhere using different names. He has 70 Facebook accounts, 20 websites and numerous YouTube pages." Magnotta actually claimed he had links to the 2006 murder of a businessman whose body parts were found under the Hollywood sign in Los Angeles.

Magnotta's mother and sister, Melissa, still lived near his granny's scruffy-red-brick house, which served as a crash pad for relatives – and was known for often being the scene of trouble. A 21-year-old cousin, Louis Yourkin – who looked up to the older Eric as a child – was in custody for drug and gun possession charges. In 2011 a blaze ripped through the house, injuring a 14-year-old, who was later charged with starting the fire. Melissa refused to talk as she scurried out of her home in front of journalists. She claimed her brother left their lives when he was 19 and returned to Toronto. Three years later, Eric had his first brush with the law. He was accused of stealing a girlfriend's credit card and using it to buy TVs, DVD players and phones. He was sentenced to nine months' jail, but charges that he sexually assaulted the girl were dropped. In his 20s he began to use a variety of exotic-sounding names and would claim to be an escort and porn star.

According to one lover, transsexual cabaret performer Nina Arsenault, he also worked as a stripper in a gay nightclub. She said Eric would often become so angry he would repeatedly punch himself in the head. She added: "He said there was some messed-up stuff that happened to him as a kid." But she found it hard to separate fact from fiction. He told her he had a baby and was in the Russian mafia. She also discovered he'd gone to a Toronto paper to deny "rumours" he was dating serial killer Karla Homolka after her release from prison. His aunt, alongside many others, believed he'd started the rumours himself. He constantly switched between male and female lovers and boasted on the web about the size of his manhood. He also uploaded a number of videos of himself torturing animals and once fed a kitten to a giant Burmese python. However, the alleged cannibal slaying left everyone reeling in shock. Criminal profiler Lee Mellor wrote a book on 60 Canadian serial killers and said that Magnotta was a "text-book" example of a child starved of affection, who went from making up stories to harming animals which ultimately led to murder. He said it was likely there were other victims waiting to be discovered. He warned: "I would not be surprised to find that Magnotta was responsible for at least one or two previous homicides."

Magnotta was flown home to Canada on 18th June 2012 on a Canadian Air Force jet as Lin's devastated family mourned the loss of their "pride and joy". He was deemed too dangerous to fly with commercial passengers. Flanked by police Magnotta was taken to court the following day in handcuffs, but he pleaded not guilty to all charges. His lawyer asked for psychological evaluations before further proceedings. Lin's decapitated head had still not been found, but it was eventually found in a park a few miles from the accused's apartment after a tip off. Meanwhile it was disclosed that a second, unedited, video made by Magnotta showed him eating his victim.

Magnotta appeared in court on 11th March 2013 charged with murder. More than 600 journalists from around the world queued from 4.00am so that they could get a seat in court. But Magnotta's lawyers wanted a full publication and media ban, meaning that only the prosecutors, judge and court clerk would know the disturbing details of the case. Lin's father was in court for the preliminary hearing, and said: "The pain of losing [a] loving son will never fade. There is nothing to [say] about Luka Rocco Magnotta. It is my duty as the father to be there." He was accompanied by a translator, although Lin's mother and sister chose to stay away from court. The trial date set by the judge was autumn 2014.

Brandon de Leon and Alexander Kinyua
(2012)

A drifter high on drugs was put in a Hannibal Lecter-style mask after threatening to eat two police officers in a cannibal attack in the United States in June 2012. Brandon de Leon was believed to have taken "bath salts" just like Rudy Eugene, who ate 75 per cent of homeless man Ronald Poppo's face in Miami in May 2012, and only stopped when police shot and killed him. De Leon (21), who had been bundled into the back of a patrol car in North Miami Beach, repeatedly slammed his head against the Plexiglas in front of him, yelling at the officers: "I'm going to eat you." At the police station he continued to growl and bare his teeth like an animal, and tried to bite the officer who was taking his blood pressure. Inside his cell, de Leon was put in leg restraints and a bite mask after he continued to bark and growl.

In a third case blamed on the zombie drug, Carl Jacquneaux (43) bit off a chunk of Todd Credeur's face in Scott, Louisiana. He only stopped after he was sprayed in the face with wasp repellant and was arrested at a nearby house. Police said this was part of a disturbing new trend where drugs were sold under the guise of household products.

In a separate cannibal case, student Alex Kinyua (21) was accused of eating the heart and brain of a family friend he killed in Joppatowne, Maryland. He murdered sex offender Kujoe Bonsafo Agyei-Kodie (37), then hid his head and his hands in tins at his family home nearby. His brother Jarrod confronted him when he found the remains, but when he returned with his dad he "observed that items were gone", the authorities said. They added: "Alex Kinyua was cleaning the container he saw them in." Detectives later found the body parts in the house, and Kinyua pointed them in the direction of a bin outside a church where the rest of the body had been dumped. He later confessed that he had eaten Agyei-Kodie's heart and brain after cutting him up with a knife, police said. The Kenyan national lived with Ghanaian Agyei-Kodie – once jailed for stalking a woman – while at Baltimore's Morgan State University in the US.

Michael Parr
(2012)

Mitchell Harrison (23), who was serving an indefinite sentence at Frankland top security jail in Durham for the rape of a 13-year-old girl, was attacked in his cell in October 2011 by Michael Parr (32). Parr pleaded guilty on 21st June 2012 to Harrison's murder. A Newcastle crown court heard him enter his plea via video link from HMP Woodhill, another top security prison where he was already serving a sentence. No other details were given during the short hearing. Mr Justice Openshaw told him: "You will be sentenced on 12th July." Nathan Mann (23) was also charged with Harrison's murder and was stated to appear in court the following month.

Harrison, originally from Wolverhampton, had apparently been held down and tortured, and was disembowelled with a makeshift blade believed to have been embedded in plastic. A jail source said the attack was like "something out of a medieval torture chamber". Harrison had been jailed in 2010 for at least four and a half years.

The two men who sliced Harrison open in order to eat his liver were told they would spend the rest of their lives in jail on 12th July 2012. Parr and Mann had cannibalistic fantasies, the court heard, and murdered Harrison in order to carry them out. They lured him into Mann's cell, where Mann first tried to strangle him and then stabbed his victim in the eye with a biro, before slashing his neck with a weapon made from plastic cutlery and razor blades. As Mann, who was serving life for murdering two elderly women, hacked into Harrison, Parr (serving life for attempted murder) held their victim down by his legs. But despite planning to remove and eat their victim's liver, they were "unable to go through with it". Both men admitted the killing. Sentencing them to life, Mr Justice Openshaw said: "Because of the risk these prisoners pose I cannot envisage the circumstances where either of them are ever released."

Cannibalization of Peter Chepongos
(2012)

A cattle herder was accused of murdering his neighbour in Tetu, Kenya, then cooking and eating his body organs. Pieces of father of five Peter Chepongos were said to have been found in a stewing pot next to a machete covered in his blood. His leg had been roasted. Mr Chepongos' family had reported him missing and his cousin, Francis Tarkus, said they had spoke to his "restless" neighbour, who denied having seen him. He added: "On the path to his house we saw blood and Chepongos' cap." The unidentified suspect, who worked as a herdsman and lived in a mud-walled hut, was due in court on 2nd July 2012 accused of murder. He was said to have confessed.

Rudy Eugene

(2012)

On 26 May 2012 Larry Vega was riding his bike along the off-ramp of Miami's MacArthur Causeway, which connects the centre of the city with the beach, when he saw a naked man chewing on the face of another man, who was also naked. At the time of the savage attack the area was packed with people going to the city's annual Memorial Day hip-hop festival.

Mr Vega told WSVN-TV in Miami: "The guy was, like, tearing him to pieces with his mouth, so I told him, 'Get off'. The guy just kept eating the other guy away, like, ripping his skin … The guy was like a zombie. It was intense. He was tearing the other man to pieces with his mouth. There was blood everywhere. It was really horrific." Mr Vega flagged down a Miami police officer, who repeatedly ordered the attacker to get off the victim. The attacker just picked his head up and growled at the officer, Mr Vega said. Armando Aguilar of the Fraternal Order of Police confirmed: "He growled at him like a wild animal and kept eating at the man's face." When the order to stop was ignored the police officer shot him. The first bullet had no effect, so the officer continued firing until the attacker was dead.

The flesh-eater was identified by the Miami-Dade County Medical Examiner's office as Rudy Eugene (31), according to Miami television station WFOR. Eugene was taken to Jackson Memorial Hospital, but a spokeswoman said the hospital would not be releasing any information about him. Miami police released few details about the attack, other than confirming that there had been a fatal shooting, but a spokesman said: "Based on the information provided, our Miami police officer is a hero and saved a life." A surveillance video camera from the nearby *Miami Herald* building captured images of the men's naked legs lying side by side after the shooting.

Mr Vega said the victim appeared gravely injured: "You couldn't really see, it was just blood all over the place." The victim fought for his life in intensive care, suffering from severe facial injuries: his attacker had bitten his eyes and chewed off his nose. Up to 80 per cent of the victim's face was affected, with the Miami hospital describing his injuries as "some of the worst staff had ever encountered".

Police had initially responded to reports of two naked men fighting on the city's MacArthur Causeway bike path. Crazed Rudy Eugene chewed off his victim's nose, ears and eyes before police gunned him down. Doctors believed that Eugene had been high on "bath salts" – a drug so called because of its appearance. Its effects can be similar to the hallucinogen LSD; a police officer said: "It can make users go completely insane." Bath salts contain the party drug mephedrone, also known as "meow meow", which was banned in Britain in 2010 and is also illegal in Australia.

Detectives said that Ronald Poppo, the 65-year-old victim, was left unrecognizable after the sickening attack. He was said to be in a critical condition in hospital. Police released a photograph of him when images claiming to show his horrific injuries emerged online. Mr Poppo remained in a serious condition at Jackson Memorial

Hospital's Ryder Trauma Center. "He had his face eaten down to his goatee. The forehead was just bone. No nose, no mouth," said Sergeant Armando Aguilar. Sergeant Javier Ortiz, vice-president of the Miami Fraternal Order of Police, said it was "one of the bloodiest and goriest scenes I've ever been to".

When the mother of the dead man dubbed the "Miami Cannibal" spoke out for the first time after the horrific flesh-eating attack, in an interview with CBS Miami, she said: "I feel devastated. He was a nice kid. He was a good kid. Everyone says he was a zombie. He was no zombie. That was my son."

Eugene's girlfriend, who remained anonymous, described him as a religious man and said she had no idea what had caused the vicious attack. She told CBS: "That wasn't him, that was his body but it wasn't his spirit. Somebody did this to him." She added that Eugene always read the Bible and his last words to her were: "I love you and I'll be back." He had kissed her goodbye and he had left, clutching his Bible. Eugene's partner believed that her God-fearing boyfriend was either drugged unknowingly or the victim of something supernatural; in her opinion, the attack was completely out of character. She suggested that Eugene, with whom she had been in an on-off relationship for five years, was possessed. Eugene's partner told the *Miami Herald* that when she discovered the naked man she had seen on TV with pieces of flesh hanging from his teeth was her boyfriend: "I thought to myself, 'Oh my God, that's crazy.' I didn't know that it was Rudy." She said Eugene had never showed any signs of violence during their relationship. There was no indication he had a history of mental illness or was using drugs other than marijuana, his girlfriend said.

In June, Eugene's girlfriend was named as Yovonka Bryant. She said that the couple often read the Bible and the Quran together, and often watched a religious television programme in the mornings. Bryant, who was questioned by police after the attack but was not under investigation, described Eugene as a Christian who wanted to know more about the Muslim faith. "He would never leave without it, his Bible, and his Quran was always by his side," Bryant said. Eugene would place the Bible on top of the Quran on the passenger seat of his car, she said. "He was just figuring out the Quran. He just really picked up the Quran and was trying to actually get into it as he was into the Bible."

Bryant had last heard from Eugene in a text message the day before the attack, but she declined to say what the message had been about. There had been no warning signs that anything was wrong with him, Bryant said during a news conference in Miami. He loved his mother and his grandmother dearly. "I felt safe with Rudy," she said. "He was happy, in a good mood. In his presence, his smile alone just uplifted my spirit ... I truly did not have a care in the world when I was with him."

It was still not clear what led to the attack on Ronald Poppo, the homeless man who remained in hospital. Poppo's family said they had had no contact with him for more than 30 years and thought he was dead. Police released few details about what might have led to the attack. Shortly before it, a person driving on the MacArthur

Causeway told an emergency dispatcher that a "completely naked man" was on top of one of the light poles and "acting like Tarzan". Surveillance video from a nearby building showed Eugene stripping Poppo, and pummelling him, before appearing to hunch over and lie on top of him.

Eugene's autopsy results were pending. His girlfriend said she thought someone may have slipped Eugene a drug, but she did not say why she thought that. Bryant, a single mother of three, said she had never seen Eugene drink and had only once saw him smoke marijuana at a party. Court records showed that Eugene had several arrests on marijuana-related charges. His brother said that Eugene sometimes smoked marijuana but didn't drink much or use hard drugs. Bryant, a billing specialist for a certified public accountant, hired celebrity attorney Gloria Allred to arrange a news conference "because she thinks it is important that the public know the truth about Rudy Eugene and her relationship with him", Allred said.

By June 2012, the mind-altering drug known as "bath salts", Narcotic Cloud Nine or Ivory Wave, which had been banned in Britain, was being blamed for a spate of cannibal attacks in America, including the attack on Ronald Poppo. Police warned people to stay away from the drug after two similar attacks were reported. The most recent had prompted an internal memo to police, warning officers that the case "bears resemblance to an incident that occurred in the city of Miami last week, when a male ate another man's face". The memo called the synthetic drug "addictive and dangerous" and said it was part of a "disturbing trend in which new drugs are sold in the guise of household products". It added: "Please be careful when dealing with the homeless population during your patrols."

The other cases being referred to where those of Brandon de Leon and Carl Jacquneaux.

The potentially addictive drug under the influence of which all these crimes were suspected to have taken place stimulates the central nervous system, and symptoms include heart palpitations, nausea, hallucinations, paranoia and erratic behaviour. It is often sold in plain packaging, with the contents purporting to be harmless. Dr Kate Wilmer, consultant cardiologist at West Cumberland Hospital, described the effects of the drug in the *Mirror* in 2010: "What we were seeing was effectively an acute paranoid psychosis which was coming on anything from 12 hours to four days after taking Ivory Wave.

"The things that were common with all of them were extreme agitation, both auditory and visual hallucinations, and paranoid delusions. The patients were extremely scared and that made some of them quite aggressive and difficult for the staff to deal with. If we tried to give them anything to help them, they were convinced we were trying to harm them, so we have had to heavily sedate two or three of them in order to treat them properly.

"Some of them had a very fast heart rate when they came in and one of them experienced chest pain when he came in. Other problems include high blood pressure, high temperature and possible cardiac problems. This particular drug may cause long-term mental health problems and should definitely be avoided. It is taking some people days to come out of the psychosis it induces ... the worry is that some people might not come out of it at all."

On 10th June, an autopsy report said that Rudy Eugene had unidentified pills in his stomach, but no human flesh. The pills found in his system would take weeks to be identified, according to the *Miami Herald*, but the man dubbed the "Miami Cannibal" might not have eaten any flesh at all. However, the autopsy did find flesh lodged between his teeth, according to reports. On 28th June it was revealed that a comprehensive toxicology test, conducted by two labs, had found no alcohol or prescription drugs in Eugene's system; the only drug present was marijuana. He wasn't high on bath salts, stated the coroner; he wasn't high on anything during the 18-minute attack. This news was welcomed by Eugene's family, who had maintained throughout that he was a peaceful, religious man who didn't touch hard drugs and only occasionally smoked cannabis. Younger brother Marckenson Charles said: "There's no answer for it, not really. Anybody who knew him knows this wasn't the person we knew him to be. Whatever triggered him, there is no answer for this."

In August, Mr Poppo spoke about the attack for the first time. In a tape obtained by CBS, Poppo told police: "He just ripped me to ribbons. He chewed up my face. He plucked out my eyes. Basically that's all there is to say about it." He later added: "He mashed my face into the sidewalk. My face is all bent and mashed up ... He was strangling me in wrestling holds at the same time he was plucking my eyes out."

Mr Poppo, who had undergone several operations at Jackson

Memorial Hospital in Florida, also praised the cops who had saved his life, saying he would have been in "worse shape" had they not acted so quickly. He told Miami police that moments before the gruesome attack Eugene, whom he had never met before, was screaming at him that he was going to die. Police believed it was a chance attack, and that Eugene had simply stumbled across Mr Poppo.

CCTV footage shows a naked Eugene walking on the pavement near a bridge at around 1.55pm. He pauses in the shade before he is seen bent over a figure, the view partially obscured by a palm tree. Eugene then rolls Mr Poppo out into the sun, and starts stripping him of his clothes before straddling him. He is then seen hunched over the man's face as he begins to eat it.

By December 2012, Mr Poppo was barely speaking and was refusing to have further surgery on his devastating injuries seven months after the attack. By this time Mr Poppo was living at Jackson Memorial Perdue Medical Center, an 11-acre 163-bed rehabilitation facility in South Miami-Dade. Although he was not speaking, long-lost relatives gave an insight into his progress seven months after the horrific attack. His sister Antoinette said her brother, known as Ronnie, never mentioned the attack or his past, but discussed his accommodation and the people who cared for him. She told the *Miami Herald*: "He says they take him outside and walk him around the place. He's glad to be there ... He doesn't really talk much at all. He says, 'Take care of yourself.' It's so sad he can't see, and has to depend on other people." She added that he told her that "his face hasn't healed yet" but that he doesn't want more surgery because "it's going to hurt".

Following the gruesome attack, a New York newspaper discovered that Mr Poppo had an adult daughter, Janice Poppo DiBello; his family said they never knew she existed. Antoinette said that Janice had tried to contact her aunts and uncles, but had made no attempt to speak to her father.

Nearly a year after he had his face chewed off, the victim of the "Miami Cannibal" was finally smiling again. As the anniversary of the bizarre attack approached, photographs were released showing Mr Poppo celebrating his 66th birthday with hospital staff. He had continued his remarkable recovery, putting on 50lbs in weight and learning to play the guitar, and "living happily and adjusting to his new life", according to staff at the centre. He continued to work with an occupational therapist, who taught him how to dress himself, feed himself, shower and shave. In a short video clip, Mr Poppo gave his heartfelt thanks to supporters who had helped keep his spirits up through the dark days.

Graham Fisher

(2012)

A 22-stone cannibal killer was having a £7,000 gastric band operation on the NHS to help him stop eating so much, the *Mirror* reported in May 2012. Graham Fisher, who had killed two women and eaten the flesh of one of them, was on a waiting list for the surgery after complaining he was overweight and unfit.

Fisher (39), also a serial sex attacker, ballooned in size after bingeing on chocolate, crisps and cakes at high-security Broadmoor Hospital in Berkshire. A source said: "It is disgusting that a killer like Fisher should be allowed gastric surgery which is paid for by the taxpayer. He showed no mercy to his victims and his decision to eat everything in front of him underlines his lack of self control. We are in the middle of a recession. The NHS should reserve gastric bands for those who deserve it."

Fisher's series of horrific crimes started in 1991 when he raped a vulnerable woman in her early 40s at her home in Bromley, Kent. The sadist was not caught and went on to kill twice in 1998. Clare Letchford (40) was found dead at her flat in Hastings, East Sussex, on 18th January. The body of Beryl O'Connor (75) was discovered at her home nearby eight days later. They had both been strangled and set on fire, and Fisher had cut flesh from Miss Letchford's arm to eat it. He was finally brought to justice after being convicted of indecently assaulting two Spanish students at knife-point in Eastbourne in May 1998.

In 2008, while at Broadmoor for the sex attacks, Fisher confessed to manslaughter over the two killings. He was given an indeterminate sentence with a minimum of 21 years. Prosecutors said he targeted lonely women to satisfy a sexually sadistic aspect to his personality. Fisher, who was classified as super-obese, bought fattening treats at the hospital shop. He worked a couple of hours a day in the hospital's kitchen garden but spent most of his time sleeping in his single cell. The source added: "Despite stuffing his face on junk food he moans that he wants to be slim, and a gastric band is his only hope."

The mother of Fisher's victim Clare Letchford reacted angrily to the news of his gastric band op. From her home in St Leonards, Sussex, widow Joyce (88) said: "It's terrible he is getting preferential treatment. There is never a day I don't think of Clare. I lost my husband in the same year she was killed and you never get over it."

Gilberto Valle
(2012)

A police officer was accused on 25th October 2012 of plotting to kidnap women before cooking and eating them. A search of Gilberto Valle's computer found he had records of at least 100 potential targets, with names, addresses and photos. Valle (28) told how he planned to rape, torture and kill his victims before dining on their body parts. The FBI intercepted web chats in which the New York City cop allegedly revealed gory details about his nightmarish plan, "straight out of a horror film". In one recipe he said: "I was thinking of tying her body to some kind of apparatus, cook her over a low heat, keep her alive as long as possible." In other exchanges, investigators said Valle talked about how to fit a woman's body into an oven and boasted he could make chloroform at home to knock a woman out. He even said how "tasty" one woman looked. Dubbed the "cannibal cop", it was revealed how Valle had used the crime database at work to draw up a list of victims, a New York court heard. He bragged to an online pal that he aimed to eat "girl meat" for Thanksgiving. He denied all the charges against him, but newspapers revealed that if found guilty he could face life imprisonment.

Towards the end of February 2012, two men in Kent had been arrested in connection with the cannibal plot trial. A Kent Police spokeswoman said: "Two men aged 57 and 30 from the Canterbury area were arrested on February 21 over suspected conspiracy offences, grooming and possession of child abuse images. The two men are on police bail. Kent Police have been in touch with law enforcement authorities in the US in relation to this investigation. We can confirm it is in relation to the Gilberto Valle case in the US." Both men were released on bail. It was alleged that they had had web chats with Valle about his cannibal fantasies. Dale Bolinger – mentioned in a later entry – was one of the men, and police were seen searching sheds at the 57-year-old's house and digging in his garden. A neighbour told journalists: "They were here the whole day. There were seven police vehicles. I could see police going into the back garden. There were two police dogs and they were looking through the garden sheds. There was another police person with a shovel. I saw him digging all the soft soil in the flower beds. I think it was soil that looked like it had been dug up recently."

Reports in the US claimed that a British internet user – using the name Moody Blues – had boasted to the New York cop he had already eaten two people, and had given Valle cannibalism tips. When Bolinger was asked about the alleged offences he replied:

"Yes, I do deny them." He was separately arrested over alleged grooming and possession of the child abuse images.

Moody Blues was said to have recommended eating a woman alive. He said: "I think of it as eating her to death. The meat isn't quite like pork, but very meaty." He was also believed to have boasted how he had eaten a "black woman and a white person" and claimed to have a recipe for haggis using human offal. Valle said he wasn't into raw meat, and the men talked of severing a woman's feet and barbecuing them in front of her while she was still alive.

Moody Blues had not been identified in Manhattan Federal Court where Valle was on trial, and US police told the court they believed the Moody Blues comments were "pure fantasy". The 30-year-old man who was also questioned remained unnamed.

Mr Bolinger was suspended from his job at Kent and Canterbury Hospital pending a police investigation. Valle, who had discussed killing his wife Kathleen and other women, continued to deny charges of conspiracy to kidnap and improper use of a police computer. The New York police officer had plotted to torture and cook his wife with a butcher in India, a court heard. He told the man he "longed to butcher and cook female meat" in an online chat the year before his trial. The butcher, identified as Aly Khan, offered to provide a place in Pakistan to kill the woman, an FBI agent testified.

FBI agent Corey Walsh told the court about chats that Valle had participated in during 2012 with a New Jersey co-defendant and two co-conspirators: a man in Great Britain and Khan. Both men posed on the internet as veterans of cannibalism who could teach Valle the skills he would need. In several emails read by Walsh, Valle seemed eager to suggest his wife as an offering to Khan, though he added: "She is a sweet girl. I like her a lot. But I will move on."

Valle suggested he could talk his wife into going on a trip to India before they took her to Pakistan, where they could gag her and take her to a basement. There he said they could hang her from her feet and take turns sexually assaulting her before slitting her throat and cooking her. "I just love the thought of stringing her upside down," Valle wrote in an email displayed to the jury. He also said he would like "to see her suffer" and "slowly roast her until she dies". The jury also heard how Valle plotted to kill and eat a former University of Maryland roommate, Andria Noble. In one exchange, the police officer said: "I want her to experience being cooked alive. She'll be trussed up like a turkey ... She'll be terrified, screaming and crying."

Valle was convicted on 12th March 2013 of plotting to commit cannibalism, following a macabre trial that subjected jurors to gruesome evidence. The officer admitted he had a fetish for talking on the internet about eating human flesh. His lawyers had urged the jury to dismiss his "weird proclivities" as the ramblings of a fantasist, but prosecutors said that an analysis of Valle's computer found he was taking concrete steps to abduct his wife and at least another five other women he knew personally. On one occasion, he had showed up near the home of one woman after agreeing to kidnap her for $5,000 for a New Jersey man, who was awaiting trial as a result of the investigation. He had also looked up potential targets on a restricted database and researched chloroform. Valle "left the world of fantasy and entered the world of reality", prosecutor Hadassa Waxman said during closing arguments. She added that Valle's arrest around Halloween the year before had interrupted a ghoulish plan to "kidnap, torture, rape and commit other horrific acts on young women".

Valle, from Queens, New York, admitted he had met friends on an extreme sexual fetish website, but claimed he intended no violence. His lawyers had insisted he was merely fantasizing and stressed no women were ever harmed. Valle, a father of a daughter himself, bowed his head and looked teary-eyed when the verdict was announced. His lawyer, Julia Gatto, said: "It's a devastating verdict for us. We poured our hearts and souls into this. The jury was unable to get past the thoughts. Obviously, the case involved thoughts that were unusual and bizarre and frankly very ugly." Valle's mother, Elizabeth, shook her head as the verdict was returned. "I'm in shock and want to be left alone," she said after her son was led away.

Valle's wife, Kathleen Mangan (27), had found disturbing emails before her husband's arrest and subsequent trial – and it was her tip-off to the FBI that led to the investigation. She testified against him during the trial, telling the court that in the emails Valle had discussed slitting her throat.

Zhang Yongming

(2012)

Zhang Yongming (57), cut up his victims and sold their remains to unsuspecting customers at a market near his home, according to state media in China. The cannibal serial killer, who sold his victims' flesh as "ostrich meat", was executed. Zhang, known as the "Cannibal Monster", was found guilty of murdering 11 people and was sentenced to death at a court hearing in July 2012. He was "escorted to an execution site and executed" on 10th January 2013, state-run news agency Xinhua said.

Horrified police were believed to have found eyeballs preserved in wine bottles and pieces of flesh hanging up when they searched Zhang's home following his arrest. He reportedly ate his victims, thought to be mainly young boys, sold their flesh and also fed some to his dog, according to The Standard in Hong Kong. Residents told local media they had seen green plastic bags hanging from Zhang's home with what appeared to be white bones protruding from the top. Zhang had been previously jailed for murder but was released from prison in 1997.

In 2012, also in China, a drunk bus driver pounced on a woman and chewed her face in another horrific "cannibal attack". The victim, named locally as Du, was driving past a bus station when a crazed man ran out into the road, climbed onto her bonnet and started hitting the windscreen. When she got out of the car and tried to escape, the man, named by police as Dong, leapt on top of her and wrestled her to the ground. Dong, a bus driver, then allegedly started chewing Du's face, biting her nose and lips, leaving her covered in blood, according to local reports.

Jérémy Rimbaud
(2013)

An ex-marine "turned into a cannibal and ate an OAP's heart and skull with beans", a court was told in November 2013. French Corporal Jérémy Rimbaud (26) was accused of smashing a 90-year-old man's head with an iron bar. The French marine, who had served in Afghanistan with British troops, turned into a predatory cannibal within 10 days of leaving the army, prosecutors said yesterday.

Rimbaud was also accused of ripping out part of the elderly man's heart and skull and eating them with beans. The soldier claimed he was "acting on messages" in his head, a court in Tarbes, southwest France, heard. Rimbaud was held in custody until his trial in 2014.

Dale Bolinger
(2013)

Dale Bolinger, a British nurse, appeared in court charged over sex offences after a FBI investigation into a cannibalism plot. The

57-year-old, said to be estranged from his wife Rosemary (55), who had cerebral palsy, was also accused of trying to poison someone with dry cleaning fluid. Bolinger, formerly from Canterbury, Kent, faced 11 charges. He was present at a preliminary hearing at Canterbury Crown Court on 25th November 2013, and the case was adjourned for a plea and case management hearing on 10th February 2014.

Kent Police arrested Bolinger on 21st February 2013 after launching an investigation earlier that year as a result of liaison with FBI officers in the United States. Seven months later, he was charged with one count of administering poison to someone, two counts of possessing an indecent photograph of a child, one count of attempting to meet a girl under 16 following sexual grooming, and seven counts of publishing an obscene article.

The alleged offences were said to have taken place between July 2010 and February 2013.

Geoffrey Portway
(2013)

A vile British man admitted to a cannibal plot to kidnap, rape, kill and eat children in his US home. Twisted Geoffrey Portway – who went by the online name of Fat Longpig as he trawled the internet for victims – planned to carry out unspeakable atrocities inside a home-made dungeon that he had built underneath his house. The story, which broke in May 2013, revealed that after confessing to the sick plan he faced 27 years in jail.

When shocked police raided the 40-year-old's home in Worcester, Massachusetts, as part of Operation Holitna in 2012, a massive two-year crackdown on paedophiles, they discovered a locked door in the basement. This led to a second door that opened into Portway's dungeon, lined with special material to muffle a child's scream. It was equipped with a steel cage, 3ft wide, 4ft long and 2ft high, and fitted with locks, scalpels, butchering kits, freezers and castration tools. It also contained a child-size coffin which housed large speakers covered in a wire mesh and exterior locks, and six metal rings inside to act as restraints. They found the place strewn with indecent images of children – and the fully equipped "torture chamber". Investigators also found bondage equipment and handcuffs. A spokesman for the US Attorney's office said: "This dungeon was described in detail by Portway as a place he intended to use to keep kidnapped children while he sexually abused them and as a place to eventually murder and cannibalize the kids." In a series of disturbing web chats, uncovered by detectives, computer programmer Portway boasted of his intention to lock up youngsters in the horrific hellhole.

Portway, a UK citizen who worked for several years in America, spent hundreds of hours in online forums under his cyber moniker – the name cannibals from the Marquesas Islands of Polynesia gave to human flesh because it tasted like sweet pork. He swapped child porn and discussed "abducting, raping, murdering and eating children". Portway used Skype to communicate with another pervert over a period of several months, asking him for help with kidnapping children.

Police said that records of the conversations revealed that the two men discussed youngsters to whom they could gain access – using their names and photos. In one conversation, the other man said it would not be hard to find out where a boy lived in Baltimore. He asked: "Question is, would you go that far to snatch him?" "I might if I could get him," Portway answered. "On just the chance of getting him, probably not. There are thousands of boys closer than that."

A forensic examination of the computers uncovered evidence of more than 4,500 trades of child pornography. Portway distributed much of it based on stated specific preferences, including videos that appeared to depict dead children and the cannibalism of children. Experts recovered more than 20,000 sick images of children from his computer. Bruce Foucart, of Homeland Security Investigations Boston, said: "Since we began this operation, a worldwide network of offenders had been, and continues to be, unravelled, including Portway. We have rescued 160 children and arrested 51 perpetrators. Portway's guilty plea should serve as a stern warning; we will investigate you, we will prosecute you and we will bring you to justice."

Portway also pleaded guilty to possessing and distributing child pornography. One of his contacts was sex offender Ronald Brown, jailed for 20 years in Florida in September 2013 for plotting to kidnap youngsters through his local church. He was said to have sent Portway a picture of a young boy with lines drawn on it to show how the body should be sliced into various cuts of meat. The pair also discussed taking a child to a rented house in the Everglades, mutilating him, eating him, then feeding the "leftovers" to alligators.

Portway wrote: "Just need to open a mortuary. Any boy who is scheduled to be cremated, disappears." Federal agents began investigating the depraved man after he was found to be discussing child rape and cannibalism on the internet. He traded his sick images and videos of youngsters being horrifically abused. In one internet conversation the computer programmer talked about children he knew – identifying them as potential victims. US Attorney Carmen Ortiz said: "Clearly, the facts of this case are very disturbing. We are grateful our law enforcement officers acted when they did."

Portway was jailed for more than 26 years in the United States in 2013. Prosecutor Stacy Dawson Belf said: "He can only claim fantasy here because he hadn't done it yet." On release, he will be extradited to the UK.

Sture Bergwall
(2013)

He was the man dubbed "Sweden's Hannibal Lecter" and one of the nation's most feared prisoners. Sture Bergwall confessed to the murders of 30 people – giving police grisly details of how he raped and ate some of his victims, including children, couples and a student. The *Mirror* wrote in August 2013: "But now, aged 63, he could be freed after 20 years behind bars after it emerged that in fact he did not kill anyone."

Bergwall, who had given himself the name Thomas Quick, admitted his supposed reign of terror after committing an armed robbery and being held at a psychiatric hospital in 1993. He was later convicted of eight murders in trials between 1994 and 2001. But in 2008, he withdrew his confessions, claiming he only made them for the attention and because of medical drugs he was on at the time. As there were no forensic or witness statements, he was granted retrials on all the cases – and in early August 2013, prosecutors dropped the last murder charge. After hearing the news, Bergwall wrote on his blog: "Today is a day of joy and a day of reflection." He had already asked for a commission to be set up to identify those responsible for "things going so wrong".

The final dropped charge was one of Sweden's longest-running murder cases, which concerned the death of a 15-year-old boy who vanished in 1976. The remains of Charles Zelmanovits were found in 1993, but forensic examinations had failed to prove that he was murdered. Convicted sex offender Bergwall began admitting to the crimes, which he had researched in the hospital's library, during counselling sessions. He confessed to murders that had taken place between 1976 and 1988, including those of Trine Jensen and Gry Storvik. He also claimed responsibility for more than 20 other murders in Sweden, Norway and Finland for which he was not tried. He often described in graphic detail how he butchered his victims and how, in at least one case, he ate body parts. Bergwall was still being held in an institution because of the bank raid, but he was to be reassessed and possibly freed.

Sweden's prosecutor General Anders Perklev said the murder confessions had not been sufficient for the convictions, and that Bergwall was to be considered for exoneration from the crimes. He said that almost all the murder cases had been handled by the same "narrow circle" of police and prosecutors, and added: "There is a lot to indicate that those in charge of the probes had become fully convinced Sture Bergwall's confessions were correct. This may have meant that circumstances pointing in the other direction were not sufficiently considered."

Bergwall had been convicted in his late teens for molesting four children and, years later, for stabbing a friend while on drugs.

"Black Jesus"
(2013)

Early in 2013 a convicted rapist, who was accused of cannibalism, was on the run after breaking out of jail with 47 others. But the cult leader known as "Black Jesus" was hacked to death by villagers in Papua New Guinea. Police said that Steven Tari was cornered while attacking a woman, with media reports stating that he had been chopped up.

Tari was also suspected of having murdered a schoolgirl in August

2013. He had thousands of followers before his imprisonment in 2010, having claimed to be the true Christ and promised his cult members great wealth. Among his disciples were dozens of sex slaves whom he called his "flower girls". His rape convictions were based on evidence that he had abused these young women.

Tari had studied to become a Lutheran pastor, but had disappeared from his theological college after disputing the Bible's teachings.

Detlev Guenzel
(2013)

The girlfriend of Wojciech Stempniewicz (59), from Hanover, believed he had been kidnapped in Dresden by Detlev Guenzel (55), whom he met on a torture, S&M and cannibalism website, said the *Mirror* in December 2013. She also believed that the man she had planned to marry had become a "cannibal" victim who was killed and allegedly partly eaten by a German policeman. But police said that Stempniewicz sent a message to Guenzel saying: "Kill me and eat me up." It was further alleged that the victim had "fantasised about being murdered and eaten by someone else since his youth". However, his partner told a German newspaper: "He never had a single fantasy about death." Polish-born Stempniewicz ran a trucking and logistics firm specializing in transporting and storing goods from Eastern Europe. The Warsaw native was educated at Gdansk University and had lived in Germany for 20 years.

Guenzel, a detective, was arrested over the gruesome 'cannibal' murder after the hacked-up body of the man he had met on the internet was found in his garden. The garden was a mass of holes: various body parts were dug up by police the day after his arrest, and the hunt continued for more remains. The suspect admitted murdering his victim after the pair chatted online on a dark website for people obsessed with cannibalism, German police said. When the businessman, from Hanover, went missing police began a search, and weeks later tracked his path using his communications with the suspected killer. The pair had met on 4th November and within hours the victim was dead, police said. Dresden head of criminal investigations Maik Mainda said: "They did not know each other personally until then."

The two men met at Dresden railway station, eastern Germany, and drove to the suspect's house in the town of Hartmannsdorf-Reichenau. When police caught up with the suspect, he admitted slashing the victim's throat, officers said. Mainda continued: "The agreement was that the killing should take place immediately. The suspect then used a knife to cause a life-threatening wound on the throat of the victim, which led to his death. The suspect has told us that he then cut the victim into separate pieces, including many very small pieces, and that he also cut through bones. The suspect then buried the body parts on the sloping lawn of his property."

The killer and victim had had extensive email, text and telephone contact since October 2013 to arrange their fatal date. Detectives believed the suspect, a handwriting analysis expert, spent five hours torturing his victim before dismembering his body and burying him. They were trying to discover whether he had eaten some body parts before burying others.

The case echoed that of Armin Meiwes.

Saverio Bellante
(2014)

In January 2014 it was reported that police believed a man cut out one of his landlord's lungs and ate it, after stabbing him to death over a chess game. Italian Saverio Bellante (34) also told detectives he ate the heart of victim Tom O'Gorman (39). A post mortem found the heart intact – but a lung was missing. Bellante appeared before a court that same month accused of the killing, and was said to have admitted to police: "I am guilty." Mr O'Gorman had been bludgeoned with a dumbbell before being stabbed, according to detectives. The horrific murder scene at Castleknock, West Dublin, was deeply upsetting for officers who attended.

The eldest of three children, Mr O'Gorman had lived at the house in the leafy suburb with his mother until she died in 2012. His father, who was a vet, had died some years earlier. The Italian man had been living in the home as a lodger as Mr O'Gorman sought to supplement his income in the months leading up to the attack. Friends and neighbours were shocked at the horror.

Father Denis O'Connor said the dead man had served at the

chapel just yards from his home. He added: "He was a lovely man, a quiet man. He was well liked. People are broken by it, devastated." Bellante, who chose to represent himself in court, was remanded in custody to appear before a Dublin court and was to undergo medical assessment.

UN Slams French Forces
(2014)

Christian militias were blamed for atrocities in the Central African Republic (CAR) civil war that had been plagued by cannibalism. French peacekeepers left Muslim fighters and their families to die unarmed at the hands of Christian militias, the United Nations said on 14th January 2014. Mass killings were carried out in the war-torn CAR despite the UN sending in 1,600 troops and the African Union 4,000. The French UN force disarmed Muslim fighters in a bid to stop the killings; but their Christian enemies used the move to carry out retaliatory attacks on troops and their families. The French peacekeepers later changed their tactics.

Fighters from neighbouring Chad, ostensibly also on peacekeeping duties, unleashed a wave of killing and looting after the Muslim rebel coalition, Seleka, seized power in the CAR, sparking revenge attacks by the Christian militia. A report came in the same week that Ouandja Magloire, known as "Mad Dog", had led a machete-wielding mob that hacked a Muslim man to death before cannibalizing the body. UN human rights spokesman Rupert Colville said that evidence showed intercommunal hatred had risen to "extraordinarily vicious levels".

The crisis sent food prices soaring, leaving many households on one meal a day and 2.6 million people in need of UN humanitarian assistance, the UN World Food Programme said in a separate report. Colville defended the French peacekeepers, despite their bloody tactical blunder: "They were obviously trying to disarm armed men, which was a good thing. There were opposition elements and even civilians who took advantage of that to attack and kill people who had been disarmed, or their dependants."

"Mad Dog"
(2014)

A vicious cannibal dubbed Mad Dog prepared to eat the body of a lynched man for the second time on 19th January 2014. Dressed in a bright yellow T-shirt, Mad Dog, whose real name is Ouandja Magloire, was seen cutting a piece off the dead man's body. He then licked the blood from the knife. The horrific scenes took place in the Central African Republic capital of Bangui. He had been wearing the very same T-shirt when he carried out a similar attack the week before. Pictures of the latest attack showed the body of a murdered Muslim man being pulled through the streets after he had been captured and killed by a baying Christian mob.

After the first cannibal incident Magloire said he was seeking "revenge" for the murder of family members. He said he had been "angry" because Muslims killed his pregnant wife, his sister-in-law and her baby. He said: "They broke down the door and cut my baby in half. I promised I would get my revenge." He described how he had seen his victim sitting on a minibus and decided to follow him. He was joined by around 20 people who became a baying mob. They forced the bus driver to stop and dragged the Muslim man out on the street, where he was beaten and stabbed before being set on fire. He said: "I stabbed him in the head. I poured petrol on him. I burned him. Then I ate his leg, the whole thing right down to the white bone. That's why people call me Mad Dog." According to eyewitnesses, no-one tried to intervene.

Between 2013 and the beginning of 2014, tit-for-tat violence, rape and looting had led to the deaths of thousands of people. Tensions between Christians and Muslims had erupted into bloody conflicts all across the country, and Transitional government leader Alexandre Ferdinand Nguendet issued a strong statement begging for calm. He warned both sides: "The holiday is over the chaos is over, the pillaging is over, the revenge is over."

Since March 2013 terrible religious sectarian violence had been on the increase. Rebels installed the country's first Muslim leader, but Michel Djotodia stepped down as president in January 2014. About 20 per cent of the country's 4.6 million population were said to have fled their homes, leading to warnings of a humanitarian catastrophe. Some of the fighting appeared to have eased after rival militiamen laid down their arms in a truce brokered by the French Army. Hundreds of Christian soldiers who joined anti-balaka groups or deserted after the rebel takeover in the week of the cannibal attack turned up for duty following an appeal from the chief of staff. CAR had huge deposits of gold, diamonds and other minerals, but had seen a succession of coups and rebellions since independence from France in 1960.

North Korea
(2014)

North Korea stood accused of crimes against its own people that were as barbaric as the atrocities carried out by the Nazis during the Second World War. Its regime was attacked for "unspeakable crimes" against humanity – including deliberate starvation, death camps, torture, state-sponsored abductions, public executions and lifelong indoctrination – in a damning 372-page report released on 17th February 2014. This was compiled by a panel of experts mandated by the United Nations Humans Rights Council, and investigators interviewed defectors in South Korea, Japan, Britain and the US to discover what they had seen and suffered in a nation where 80,000 to 120,000 people are held in political prison camps.

President Kim Jong-un could now face charges at the International Criminal Court for abuses that include drowning babies, roasting torture victims over open fires, forcing abortions and exterminating families.

Michael Kirby, the retired Australian judge who chaired the panel, described the allegations as similar to those levelled at the Nazis. "It brings back memories of the end of the Second World War, and the horror and the shame and the shock," he said. The report is the most detailed probe undertaken into the warped Kim regime, which has had an iron grip over North Korea for six decades.

During the late 1990s, millions starved, or were forced to eat tree bark or grass to survive. The dossier even claims North Koreans resorted to cannibalism and the sale of "human meat" in a bid to survive. It says: "Testimonies of the sale of human meat almost disappeared after 2000. However, in 2006 there was a re-emergence in testimonies of cannibalism attributed to the economic breakdown and food shortages." One witness, known only as Mrs C, testified: "My father, because of malnourishment, passed away early in the morning of February 16, 1996. In April 1997 my older sister and younger sister died of starvation. In 1998, my younger brother died."

Mothers abandoned or killed their babies at birth because they could not feed them. Around 1997, then leader Kim Jong-il ordered military families to adopt abandoned children. Those that did were considered heroes. The military in the Communist regime were accused of stealing food but ordinary people were dealt the harshest of punishments if they stole. One woman testified that she witnessed five public executions during the famine – all shot in the head. The regime's iron grip on power meant that thousands were sent to prison camps. Three generations of a family were often jailed for political offences if one member was deemed guilty – often with no reason given. A witness called Kim Hye-sook said she spent 28 years from the age of 13 in such a camp, only to find on release that the family had been punished because her grandfather fled to the Republic of Korea during the Korean War. Former detainee Shin Dong-hyuk was also 13 when he reported a conversation he overheard between his mother and brother in which they talked about escaping from the camp. He had to watch as they were executed. Within months he was tortured – hung over a fire until his back was burned.

Sexual violence is common in the camps. Witness Ahn Myong-chol said the commander of a state security department unit raped a woman, who became pregnant and gave birth to a baby. The mother and her child were taken to the detention and punishment block, where the baby was thrown in the feeding bowl for the dogs. Another witness saw guards take the baby of a mother at the Onsong County detention facility moments after it was born and drown the child in a bucket. Officials thought the mother had slept with a Chinese man and said of the baby: "It doesn't deserve to live." In another detention centre a witness saw a mum forced to suffocate her child moments after giving birth.

A *Mirror* journalist at the border uncovered the true story of North Korea that warmongering Kim Jong-un did not want the outside world to see. "A child of around 10 sits dying of starvation by the side of the road, while just yards away soldiers load enough rice on to trucks to feed families for weeks.

"As the young boy slumps on the grimy kerb in his filthy, oversized army jacket, locals stroll past zombie-style without even glancing in his direction or displaying an ounce of pity for his wretched plight.

"Nearby his friends scavenge in disease-ridden rubbish tips for scraps of what might pass for food in a land where people are so poor they are forced to eat even corpses, according to those on the inside. And not far away, prisoners are herded from their harsh labour camps to frantically dig out crops from frozen ground while trigger-happy troops hover over them waiting for the one wrong move that could end with death. This was the real North Korea in 2013 – the one that warmongering leader Kim Jong-un did not want the outside world to see. And the vision of hell is a far cry from the Stalinist propaganda pictures peddled out in April 2013 showing smiling people hailing their great leader as if they are the happiest folk around in a land where all is rosy."

The images, taken by brave campaigners desperate to reveal the truth of Kim's brutal regime, were handed to the *Mirror* as William Hague warned Pyongyang it faces harsher sanctions if it goes ahead with a fourth missile test. Speaking at a G8 summit in London, the Foreign Secretary said: "If the DPRK conducts another missile launch or nuclear test we have committed ourselves to take further significant measures.

"We don't specify what those further significant measures are but clearly what we're talking about is in the field of sanctions." Mr Hague spoke as North Korea moved a missile launcher into position with a range of 2,180 miles amid fears it was training weapons on the US, Japan or Guam.

Dictator Kim continued to ignore the plight of his starving people, while making sure the army was well stocked with food as he sent them to the front line in preparation for war with South Korea.

Near the starving boy – secretly filmed at Yang Gang county, near the Chinese border – bags bursting with food were being hauled on to vehicles destined for the potential battle zones along with the soldiers and millions of pounds worth of weaponry. Among them were well-dressed young women in high heel boots. The *Mirror* journalists watched the shocking footage of the misery Kim's regime was inflicting with Pastor Kim Seung-eun, a cleric who had helped more than 1,000 North Koreans flee.

Speaking at his home in the South, he said: "There are people in North Korea who are so hungry they have turned to cannibalism. One man was shot dead, executed, because he ate half of another human being and sold the rest as meat. People are living like animals in that country.

"I do what I can to get as many out as possible but it is very, very dangerous, especially for the people on the inside who help me. The person who filmed the footage of the boy focused on him for a reason. Someone had told him this boy was dying by the side of the road and he went looking for him.

"It is very distressing. Very upsetting, but I hope the world will be shocked by this footage and help more refugees and defectors to escape that dreadful place."

The 48-year-old reverend had been sneaking defectors out of the North for several years, often bribing hungry border guards and officials for help. It could cost him £5,000 in planning, rations, bribes for border guards, train and boat tickets. He had also helped bring out video images like the ones of the dying boy. They were filmed by critics of the regime who faced certain death if caught. Pastor Kim said: "I cannot tell you if I have been inside, to go to North Korea for South Koreans would be a huge crime.

"But I have friends who take the camera back inside and film the real truth of North Korea. It is important people realise how bad it really is in there."

The images showed how dehumanized North Koreans have become under the Communist government. Human beings who could walk past children starving to death did so because they themselves did not have a scrap of food to help – it had seemingly become the norm. They were used to a daily diet of death and it had clearly hardened their senses. One piece of footage showed a border guard pointing his machine gun down the lens of the cameraman after he had been spotted. The man had been filming from across the Chinese border. As the guard raised his weapon and takes aim, the snapper flees for his life, screaming in alarm.

These scenes were a world away from the polished streets and tiled walls of the capital Pyongyang from where its elite ruled with a murderous iron fist. In another of the films the near-tree-less countryside comes into view and the camera zooms in on a male and female gulag – a desolate prison in Haesan. Men and women were seen clawing at the solid ground to get at the crops, no doubt destined for the army and Kim Jong-un's cronies. The prisoners were marched out of a labour camp – by soldiers wearing North Korean

Army uniforms. A painted sign on the entrance supports Kim and a red star emblem flies above. They were forced to carry logs to rebuild a small footbridge and were also seen smashing up rocks.

Pastor Kim said: "Many years ago I went to the border between China and North Korea and I will never forget the poverty, so I decided to do something about it. This was some of the most dangerous footage ever taken inside North Korea. It is impossible to make North Korea look attractive except in Pyongyang. This is the horror truth of the countryside."

The sight of people doing forced labour echoes what many people have told the *Mirror* journalists. "We have also been told of children being left to die in the street. They were often orphans whose parents had been killed. During the years of severe food shortages this happened a lot. The guards told them they were not allowed to do anything to help out. The labour camp the journalists were talking about was a police facility.

"It was quite likely that the people they could see had not been convicted of serious crimes; it might be simply a case of going into China to make some money or find some food. They were then detained as soon as they got back into North Korea and put into prison. What happened at Hyesan was that men and women were strip-searched when they are back inside North Korea. There was very limited food and they used food as a punishment. If one team of labourers did not fulfil its quota of work they did not get that day's food ration. The journalists were alerted to many people starving to death and others suffering from severe malnutrition. There were many horrific stories emerging from North Korea that the smuggled films would appear to back up. Women who had gone into China to find money for their families were sexually exploited by the guards on their way back in. If anyone made a mistake they were brutally punished. There were arbitrary executions. Sometimes people were tortured for a perceived mistake."

The *Mirror* reporters could see people in one film involved in mining and breaking rocks under the supervision of an armed guard. They were definitely in chain gangs. It was very typical of the reports they received. One wrote: "As can be clearly seen, control is exercised by the guards and the people have no rights, no money and often no food. At the end of the day they are then returned to huge prison detention centres, in horrific conditions."

A nurse who defected from leader Kim Jong-un's regime just three months before the news article in April 2013 spoke to a *Mirror* reporter who sent back devastating news of the horror from the border. The sickening routine she endured was heralded by the loud horns of North Korean Army trucks, followed by the hammering of fists and boots on nearby neighbours' doors. Pistol-wielding security thugs would line-up villagers, insisting their children stood still and waited for the most obscene street show on Earth.

They would then watch in horror as a soldier dragged out a weeping suspect, who would then be shot in the back of the head at point-blank range. Choi Eun-ok, the nurse who defected to the South from the terrifying regime, recalled the horror with a blank expression. The translator could barely hear her as she was so used to whispering through fear of eavesdropping spies misinterpreting her conversations.

She said: "I saw hundreds of executions between 1998 and 2005, perhaps as many as three in one week and all of them in the street in front of me and my family. This period was when we saw the most regular executions, between 1998 and 2005, when it became really bad. Everyone in the village – children and adults – were forced to watch."

Mrs Choi, 54, fired the journalist a stern look that emphasized the importance of what she was about to say. She continued: "Both of my children saw the executions because the soldiers insisted. They want to convince everyone at a very early age that they have to obey and they have to witness what will happen if they do not obey.

"I had no choice – each time they came to our home and ordered us all to bring out our children to watch people getting executed." What she then tells the journalist exposed the level of cruelty the security forces will descend to as they create a climate of fear. She said: "The soldiers would shoot the people whilst the victims were wearing thick clothes to keep out the cold. At least this meant we would not have to see too much blood. But after 1998 they wanted to make the killings more horrifying for us and scare us into not disobeying the system so they forced victims to come out in thinner clothing.

"We could see so much blood. It made us much more fearful." It was a measure of how the barbaric system made civilians grateful for small mercies when she held her head in her hands and said quietly: "It seems awful but somehow killing people in thick clothes seemed less cruel. When they started shooting people in thin clothes sometimes my children would not be able to eat for days they were so disturbed by the executions.

"It was terrible. In recent years there has hardly been any food anyway."

Slightly built Mrs Choi was sitting in the home of Pastor Kim Seung-Eun, 48, whose church, The Caleb Mission, had helped more than 1,000 defectors and refugees escape the hell of North Korea. At this point she lived in a bustling South Korean town outside the capital Seoul but even then she had not escaped the immense cruelty of the place she fled. She had spent most of her adult life with her husband and latterly their two children, a boy and a girl, in the poor town of Gyung Seong, north east of Pyongyang, close to the Chinese border. Some years ago her son died in a fishing accident, she said. But she fled North Korea to find her daughter, who had recently crossed the border to China. Sadly she learned her daughter had fallen into the hands of Chinese gangsters who sold her on. She had heard nothing about her since. Many shady human-trafficking gangs had emerged on the North Korea-China border who sold young girls into prostitution. To search for her daughter, Mrs Choi slipped into China past border guards who were bribed. But she could find no trace of the girl after several weeks. Finally Pastor Kim Seung-Eun, a prolific campaigner, helped to bring Mrs Choi to Seoul. There he helped her settle while he and his contacts investigated the girl's whereabouts, which in the spring of 2013 remained a mystery.

When asked about her husband, Mrs Choi shook her head, stared at the floor and said: "He is still there." She wept as she told the journalist: "Now I know I have escaped that place and I feel I am safe here but where are my family? My husband and my daughter – I have nothing. I have nothing." In order to protect family members still stuck in North Korea, the *Mirror* agreed not to publish details about the woman's husband and changed her name.

Most of the 25,000 North Koreans who had fled to the South since the 1953 armistice still feared the regime's ruthless network of spies operating in the region were trying to track them down. Defectors hoped that if it was not known they were in South Korea then they will be labelled "missing presumed dead" and remaining relatives would be left alone.

During her life in the North, Mrs Choi had seen many of her friends and neighbours disappear over the years. She said: "You never knew when you were talking to a friend or simply someone you knew, who was a spy. There were spies everywhere. You talk to a family member one day and that person could be working for the security people and tell them what you said.

"If it was thought harmful to the country or you said anything about Kim Jong-il when he was alive or Kim Jong-un now you'd disappear. Sometimes we saw security people come for them and they would be taken off to prison. One year the father of a family we knew was taken to one of the two prisons in our area and nobody knew why. A year later the security men came and their entire home was emptied of furniture, belongings and clothes. And then the rest of the family, wife and children, were taken away. We never saw them again."

The two main prison camps in the area included Camp 21 and 22, the latter of which was a notorious gulag where many inmates had been killed or died of ill-treatment. Mrs Choi confirmed she had heard of both jails and they were in the area where she once lived. It was feared that as many as 400,000 prisoners in North Korea had died in labour camps in the past 30 years and many were killed by biological or chemical experimentation. Even though she was safer and had access to food Mrs Choi was thin and looked underfed but when she fled North Korea she weighed just six stone. She had put on a stone since her defection. Occasionally sobbing, she said: "Every day was a struggle to get food. As a family we were able to live on one meal a day but it was never enough for us. I gained weight when I moved to the South and thankfully I feel reasonably healthy physically. But I think of my family. I have my freedom but I don't really have it as I cannot be free until I know what happened to them. I think of them all of the time."

Anesson Joseph
(2014)

A naked man with "superhuman strength" was shot dead by police after attacking a retired police officer, a father and son and a teenage boy in a drug-fuelled rampage. Officers attempted to Taser 6ft 3in 250lb Anesson Joseph, who witnesses said was growling like a wild animal, but were unable to subdue him. The 28-year-old suspect also bit the face of his teenage victim in the attack, which bore chilling similarities to that of Miami cannibal Rudy Eugene.

The shocking incident happened at around 8.30pm in March 2014 in Palm Beach County, Florida, according to Sheriff Ric Bradshaw. Naked Joseph, who was believed to have been under the influence of hallucinogenic drugs, began chasing retired New York police officer Douglas Kozlik (66), who was out for his nightly walk. The victim was rushed to Delray Medical Center with serious injuries, but was released from hospital the following day.

Joseph then chased a man and his 10-year-old son, injuring the child, before attacking 18-year-old Tony Grein and his 16-year-old sister Tania as they took out rubbish.

The teenager had a box cutter on him and tried to defend himself as Joseph bit his face, but the assailant was "ridiculously strong". Tony told the *Palm Beach Post*: "He started biting right away, not a punch, not a hit like you would expect. I was kind of shocked." The young man said Joseph appeared to be unable to feel pain, even as he was stabbed in the face with the box cutter. Tony added: "It was that fear of, 'This guy is invincible.'"

"He's obviously delirious on something," Sheriff Bradshaw said. "He is a huge guy. He takes a fighting stance. They're trying to get him on the ground. He starts charging them. The Taser did not affect him." At that point, an officer fired three shots, one to the torso and two to the lower part of Joseph's body. He was rushed to hospital but died a short time later.

Bradshaw told the newspaper: "We don't know right now if he's expired from the gunshots, or if he's expired because of obviously he's on some type of drugs that have made him act like this [*sic*].

"There's no way to know if those are the shots that actually killed him, or if he's died from what they called excited delirium. He's obviously on some type of narcotics to make him act like this."

Was Michael Rockefeller Cannibalized?

(2014)

Michael Rockefeller was killed when researching head-hunting Asmat people in New Guinea, according to claims reported in the *Mirror* in March 2014. As heir to one of America's richest dynasties, Michael Rockefeller should have lived out his days sipping champagne at society parties. But in 1961, he disappeared, and for more than half a century his fate has remained a mystery.

Now, after painstaking worldwide research, writer Carl Hoffman is sure he knows what happened. On a savage coast thousands of miles from his lavish New York home, the 23-year-old Harvard graduate, great-grandson of the world's richest man, was butchered and eaten by cannibals. Says Hoffman: "Even though he was the son of incredible wealth and power, at that moment he was probably the least powerful person on earth."

Michael had gone with anthropologist René Wessing to study the culture of the head-hunting Asmat people in the former Dutch colony of New Guinea when their catamaran capsized on 21st November 1961. They were 10 miles offshore and after waiting in vain for a passing ship, Michael decided to swim for it. Wessing was later rescued but Michael vanished. For more than half a century the Rockefellers insisted he had drowned, but rumours circulated that he had been eaten by wild animals. Some even said he'd made it to the shore and gone native. But Hoffman's research offers compelling evidence that he was killed and eaten by the Asmat. After studying the accounts of priests and a Dutch patrolman in the Netherlands, archives and interviewing tribesmen related to the killers, he has built up a gruesome picture.

His new book *Savage Harvest* describes how he claims Michael survived the shark and crocodile-infested sea only to be tortured, beheaded and devoured by tribesmen. Describing the man who began the onslaught he writes: "He howled and arched his back and drove his spear into the white man's floating ribs. Michael screamed, groaned a deep, inhuman sound. With one blow of an axe in the back of his neck, Michael Rockefeller was dead."

After hacking off his head the cannibals chanted while smearing his blood on their own bodies then expertly carved the young man into pieces. Following an established ritual, they broke his ribs with an axe, ripped out his entrails and cut off his arms and legs.

"Pieces of meat were placed in the fire ... they pulled the charred legs and arms out of the fire, tore the meat off the bones and mixed it with crumbly light grey sago for everyone to eat," says Hoffman. The head was a prized trophy and the brains, scooped out of a hole in the skull, were a delicacy reserved for the tribal elders. "There really are no alternative explanations," says Hoffman. "You'd have to go to great lengths and come up with much more convoluted explanations to account for them not killing him. If you look at all the evidence and details and if you understand Asmat cultural practices it all fits together. All the proof is in documents which anyone can see."

The tribe involved had met Michael just days earlier. Their village of Otsjanep was one of 13 he visited with René Wessing and local guides while exploring a civilization which had been isolated for more than 40,000 years until 20 years earlier. The brutal act of murder when they caught him alone was revenge for a recent attack by Dutch colonists. Michael was just "in the wrong place at the wrong time" says the author. Catholic missionaries were trying to stamp out head-hunting and cannibalism but in 1961, Asmat customs still involved eating human flesh, swapping wives and drinking urine in bonding rituals. The Dutch authorities did not want a spotlight shone on this behaviour.

"The fact that he was murdered by these cannibals was inconvenient," says Hoffman. "The Dutch and the Catholic church there had to cover it up."

Michael's disappearance shocked and mystified America because the Rockefellers, giants of industry, banking and politics, were treated like royalty.

The family were behind the creation of New York City landmarks including the United Nations building, the Museum of Modern Art and the World Trade Center.

Michael was the great-grandson of oil tycoon John D Rockefeller. His father Nelson, US vice-president under Gerald Ford, was governor of New York at the time of his disappearance. In fact, Michael was in New Guinea in the first place to bring back artefacts for the New York Museum of Primitive Art which his father had founded in 1957.

"People who are incredibly rich and powerful are supposed to be in control of their destiny," says Hoffman. "When something happens that shows them to be human like the rest of us there is something fascinating about that."

After his disappearance Michael's father and his twin sister, Mary, now 75, travelled to New Guinea to launch an extensive search. But no body or even a scrap of his clothing was ever discovered, though a gasoline can, similar to the one Michael used during his swim to shore, was later picked up by the Dutch Navy. "The family haven't ever entertained any possibilities of what happened to Michael other than him drowning," says Hoffman. "I have actually been in contact with Mary in the last six weeks. She didn't say much but she did state again that for them it's a private matter. There's no concrete forensics and no body was ever recovered so we can never say with complete certainty what happened to Michael Rockefeller. But no one can claim I'm making this up. My research is watertight. Besides, you couldn't make this story up – the truth is literally stranger than fiction."

Meanwhile, the Asmat tribe are still living in the same area in the south west of Indonesian New Guinea. They gave up cannibalism many years ago.

Cannibal Killers